T0284049

Critical Acclaim for Beth Kaplan

"*Midlife Solo* shapes bright fragments from a remarkable life into a twenty-first century kaleidoscope of women's experience."

CHRISTOPHER MOORE,
twice past president of the Writers' Union of Canada

"Beth Kaplan has a magnificent gift for stories that are sad, at times heartbreaking, and stories that are increasingly joyful. Great soul food all round.

DR. K. BELICKI, professor of psychology, Brock University

"She writes about a huge diversity of experiences and situations with such intelligence, compassion, and humour that the specific becomes universal."

CURTIS BARLOW, former Canadian cultural diplomat in Washington and London

"This book is wonderful. Kaplan expresses beautifully the most meaningful aspects of a life she makes a point of enjoying to the hilt."

ANNE FRANCIS, Editor, *Canadian Running*

"Beth is a terrific writer; I am so impressed. And what a life!"

ABIGAIL THOMAS, *New York Times* bestselling author

"Such a joy to read Beth's words again. Clear and strong through calamity and reflection, they wind around us and draw us in."

TOM ALLEN, CBC host, musician, author, producer

"Perfect pieces, poignant and touching, full of insight and honesty. They capture yearning, ambivalence, disappointment and sometimes victories, and the pain and glory of love."

ROSALIND GILL, author, professor

"Riveting. Beautifully written, full of heart, funny and thought-provoking."

ROBIN PACIFIC, author, visual artist

"I was riveted by Beth Kaplan's words of wisdom and humour. She expressed those moments in her life so eloquently."

DIANA LEE, trans writer

MIDLIFE SOLO

MIDLIFE SOLO

writing through chaos
to find my place in the world

Beth Kaplan

Library and Archives Canada Cataloguing in Publication

Title: writing through chaos to find my place in the world : essays / Beth Kaplan.

Names: Kaplan, Beth, 1950- author.

Identifiers: Canadiana (print) 20230511538 |
            Canadiana (ebook) 20230524478 |

ISBN 9781771617321 (softcover) | ISBN 9781771617338 (PDF) |
ISBN 9781771617345 (EPUB) |

Classification: LCC PS8621.A615 M53 2023 | DDC C814/.6—dc23

Published by Mosaic Press, Oakville, Ontario, Canada, 2023.

MOSAIC PRESS, Publishers
www.Mosaic-Press.com
Copyright © Beth Kaplan, 2023

All rights reserved. Without limiting the rights under copyright reserved here, no part of this publication may be reproduced, stored in or introduced into any retrieval system, or transmitted in any form or by any means—electronic, mechanical, by photocopy, recording or otherwise—without the prior written permission and consent of both the copyright owners and the Publisher of this book.

Printed and bound in Canada.

MOSAIC PRESS
1252 Speers Road, Units 1 & 2, Oakville, Ontario, L6L 5N9
(905) 825-2130 • info@mosaic-press.com • www.mosaic-press.com

Author's note: Many of the essays that appeared in print or were read on the radio have been substantially rewritten, and the titles used here are often not the titles in the original. A few names have been changed to protect privacy.

CONTENTS

CONTENTS

PREFACE:
TELLING TRUE STORIES

O n a nightmarish day in September 1990, it all came apart. My marriage of ten years had been disintegrating; that day, he and I finally separated, and he moved out. Our traumatized children were six and nine.

What now? How would I cope or earn a living? I'd spent my twenties as a professional actress in Vancouver and my thirties as a stay-at-home wife and mother in Ottawa and Toronto, had recently earned an MFA in Creative Writing and wanted to become a writer. Now here I was, a forty-year-old single mother about to enter a dreadful period of hostilities with my ex, fought through our lawyers. I had no notion how to manage on my own, let alone embark on a bewildering new career.

But eventually, in a powerful gesture of mutual good-will, he and I made peace. He agreed to pay the mortgage on our family home and provide some spousal support as well as child support. And he was as good as his word.

Maybe I would cope, after all.

Not long after the settlement, a former colleague from my acting days ran into me at the Y and went on about her upcoming TV series and season at Stratford.

"And you, Beth," she asked, feigning interest, "what are you doing these days?"

What could I say? I was very busy — volunteering, looking for paid work, in intensive therapy, doing research whenever possible on a book, delving occasionally into dating. But mostly, my days were crammed with children and house, house and children.

"I'm researching a big biography of my great-grandfather, a Yiddish playwright once known as the Jewish Shakespeare," I said, a tentative boast.

"Still? That's what you said last time we talked, years ago," she replied.

I felt utterly pathetic.

What I was doing with my life, besides raising kids, was invisible; it would be years before the book was finished. My previous work had been in the boisterous, communal, structured workspace of the theatre, with a director and fellow actors, the clear deadline of opening night, instant feedback from an audience. How to launch a new kind of job that meant sitting alone in a room with my thoughts and my pen — and little remuneration, if any?

I had no idea, no time, and no confidence. With nothing published, I could not call myself a writer. Who was I now to the outside world but an unemployed single mother? Looming behind me were my father, a brilliant scientist and high-profile social activist, his brother my uncle, the even more brilliant world bridge expert, and my great-grandfather, the renowned playwright. And in some ways even more daunting, my clever, artistic mother, who'd devoted her life and considerable skills to her family. The weight of family expectations was crushing.

So what was the logical thing for this solo woman to do, to fill her almost non-existent down time, bring in the big bucks, and make herself visible to the reading world?

Why, write essays, of course!

One morning, reading the *Globe and Mail*'s Facts and Arguments column, a thousand-word personal essay open to everyone, I thought, *Here's the place to start*. Snatching bits of time, I worked on an essay about my kids and, with trepidation, sent it in; to my joy, it appeared in the paper only a few weeks later. Even more amazing, the *Globe* sent a cheque for a big fat $100. Friends got in touch. They'd read it. They said they liked it.

After the long hard slog of the biography, which I'd spent over ten years researching in complete obscurity and which would require ten years more, the speed of this publication was miraculous. From then on, when something interesting happened, or an important scene from my past floated up into the light, I sat when I could to craft another essay, and many, to my gratification, were published in newspapers and then in magazines. I began to read other new pieces regularly on CBC radio. That was the best of all, working simultaneously as both writer and actor.

Essays were so much easier than the book. They were brief, possible to write in snatches of time, and appeared in print or on air so soon after writing, the swift response from readers felt almost like applause. This former actress enjoyed that.

And the pieces were current; as someone who has kept a diary since the age of nine, it came naturally to me to chronicle day-to-day stresses, observations, joys. Part of me is always watching, preparing to tell the story. The kids got used to appearing, warts and all, in the newspaper. Nothing was ever published about them without their permission, but they liked the notoriety. My young son, after we'd had a moving heart-to-heart talk one day, asked plaintively, "Mum, is this going to appear next week in the *Globe*?"

An acquaintance from what is now Toronto Metropolitan University hired me to teach nonfiction writing. It was clear what the course should cover: how to shape the truth of a life in personal essays and memoir.

Where was my actress friend now? Though the book was still inching along, this homemaker was emerging as a public voice. So many pieces eventually appeared in the *Globe*, an acquaintance thought it was my personal column.

This was what I could contribute, outside the kitchen.

And so from my forties to my sixties, through the nineties and into the aughts, I wrote scores of mostly short essays, stopping finally to focus on writing books instead. Until then, the satisfaction of chronicling one single mother's tumultuous journey through midlife was immense.

It was years before I reread them and thought, these still have a lot to say.

Personal essays allow us to struggle on paper with our deepest questions, said writer Mary Pipher, *and then to share that struggle with others.*

The morning an essay about my divorce was published in the *Globe*, my phone rang. It was a man in another city who'd tracked down my number. He was in tears.

"Your essay — I don't know how you knew, but that's me," he said, his voice trembling. "That's my divorce."

But it wasn't; it was my divorce. And yet it was his too.

If you tell your own small story candidly and well, it will matter. That is the hope of essay writers.

That is my hope.

THE BREAK

If we don't believe in the future we are planning, the house we are mortgaged to, the person who sleeps by our side, it is possible that a tempest (long lurking in the clouds) might bring us closer to how we want to be in the world.

Deborah Levy

ANNOUNCEMENT

"I think we should call it quits," he says.

We are sitting in the living room watching a miracle on television: the provincial election is over, and the NDP has won Ontario. Bob Rae is our new premier. My husband and I, both NDP supporters, are overwhelmed by this victory.

Overwhelmed by the failure of our marriage.

At that moment, he says he has decided to move out. I know I've pushed him to this unbearable decision. Lately, suffocating under the burden of our misery, I can hardly function. We cannot pretend or lie anymore. Whatever made us love one another with the glorious passion of the first year, and the second and third and fourth and even the fifth, now, five years later again, that feeling is gone. Everything about him enrages me. He must feel the same.

Balloons on the TV, confetti, Bob Rae making a beautiful speech, left-wingers rejoicing in the triumph of the people, the workers, against the fat cats. In a living room in downtown Toronto, one small couple is choosing to slice everything in two — home, children, finances, hearts.

The children are asleep upstairs, with no idea what they will awaken to find. We turn off the TV and go to bed, strangers, he on one side and I on the other, the gulf between our backs as wide and cold as a frozen river of ice.

Sleep comes for him but not for me. In the morning the front page of our newspaper blares out the news: "NDP Triumphs!"

In the kitchen, he and I are preparing to tell our children.

Eric and I had begun dating eleven years before, in December 1979. I'd returned to Vancouver from a five-month adventure in France to find that a colleague I liked a lot had just ended his marriage. I was twenty-nine and eager to change my life, and here he was, the ideal man, smart, kind, handsome, and extremely hard-working, injured by love and needing comfort. Only a few months after our first date, we were living together. A few months after that, I got pregnant.

All was bliss. At our daughter Anna's birth, a delivery room nurse was moved to tears by the powerful love so evident between us. Our happiness carried us through various upheavals, especially when Eric's dedication to his career led him to attempt an MBA at night while handling a gruelling workload by day. I gladly quit my acting career to take care of the three of us and, part time and then long distance, to earn an MFA in Creative Writing.

When our daughter was two, my husband was offered an important job on the other side of the country. We'd spent only a couple of years in the small city where our son was born when he was given another huge promotion, this time in Toronto. I struggled to settle our young family and ace my job as wife to a fast-rising arts executive.

Eric's workaholic tendencies were exacerbated in a workaholic metropolis. Before long, to my disbelief, he took a second big job on top of the first. Absorbed in his demanding new worlds, he was almost never home, while I, two moves away from work contacts, friends, and family, did my best to become the angel in the kitchen.

He made the money, and I did everything else.

In September 1986, we managed to buy our own house, a narrow Victorian semi-detached that needed a huge amount of work we could not afford to do. I was now — how had this happened? — a stay-at-home mother with two small children, a roof that leaked, and a basement that flooded. I threw myself into the huge task of renovation and repair, while he continued to work long and hard to pay for it all. Providing is what Eric's background had trained him to do, and he did it well. But, much more than money, I wanted his time and attention, the gentle playfulness I'd liked so much in him, that rarely showed itself now.

And he'd married a sunny, accomplished woman who was now engulfed in the endless, tedious demands of homemaking. Year by year, Eric and I were becoming our worst selves — he sacrificing all for his work; I, buried and lost.

In July 1988 my father died, and this massive loss intensified my internal crisis. There was poison in the air. In the end, the disconnect became unbearable.

In the end, it was I who chose to be free of a heavy, unyielding weight.

He sits there, the man I once loved so fiercely there was no room to love anyone else. But here they are, walking into the room, the two I love so very much more: my daughter, nine, dark hair and eyes like my dad's side of the family, snub nose, soft moon face; my son, a sturdy six-year-old, tall and blonde with blue eyes like his dad. Their father and I are at the kitchen table in the cool September light.

"Sit with us, kids," he says. "We have something to tell you."

My daughter's eyes know. She knows everything; she's been called an old soul. My son knows nothing except that there is tension here and has been for a long time.

Their father is pale and stern. My face must be white with strain. My stomach is heaving; I want to vomit. I want to be anywhere but this room, the warm comfortable kitchen of a home that is about to be forever ripped apart.

"My darlings," I start, trying to catch my breath, "you know your dad and I love you more than life itself."

What does that mean? They sit looking at us, her black eyes focused, tense, boring into mine, his blue eyes puzzled, confused.

"But sometimes grownups grow apart," I go on. "Sometimes mummies and daddies need some time away from each other."

My son starts to cry. We are never going to recover from this. We will go down. It's his fault. It's his fault. It's my fault. We will never recover.

"I have a new place to live, a cool apartment," my husband says with forced cheer. "It's really really close by. I'll see you all the time."

I want to murder him. He wants to murder me. When will it be over, the agony of this death? What's happening here will scald my soul forever as the most harrowing episode of my life, and perhaps theirs too.

Is it too late to change our minds?

We will not change our minds, and our crying children will not change them for us. He will move out, and I will be heartbroken, and crushed by guilt, and very, very relieved.

Our children will just be heartbroken.

IN THE SMALL ROOM

'll be in the small room again today.

I'm going to see my mentor and confidante — my psychoanalyst. A trusted guide, a wise older woman hired to think about me, to help me figure myself out. I recount tales from my tumultuous past and turbulent present. She listens and asks questions, and helps me see clearly what was happening then, what it means now. Helps me understand who I was and why, who they were and why, how we got here.

She listens.

I first went to her toward the end of my marriage, saying, "Everything's fine, just a few little things to discuss," expecting her to pat me on the head and send me on my way. When she heard the few little things, she urged me to return.

Her calm voice tried to keep me with my husband and then guided me as, drowning in loss and pain, I navigated through the first days, the first weeks and months of this frightening new solo life. I clung to my time with her as to a life raft of sanity. My biggest concern at first was that as our lives were blowing up, my children had endured a distracted, neglectful mother. I was determined to be a much better parent than my parents, but the guide map of my own upbringing was, to say the least, faulty.

How to do this most vital of jobs with no idea how to do it? How to make sense of my background with any degree of objectivity?

She said, "You should come more often than once a week." I was reluctant. Cost and time were two huge worries, but need, too. Was that much therapy really necessary?

Yes, yes it was. I ended up seeing her twice a week, then three times, and eventually, by the year after the separation, four times a week. This was full-scale psychoanalysis; she reduced her fee to make the commitment possible, and I started to buy our clothes, gifts, and household items at Goodwill.

Still, suspicious of the process, for a year I resisted lying down on the couch. When you sit facing her, you're chatting with an advisor. When you lie down, you're a client or, worse, a patient.

But now I'm not ashamed. My beleaguered self needs the support of an expert medical professional. She's healing me as surely as the doctor did who set my sprained arm or prescribed antibiotics for an infection. She is a doctor who's healing me, but she's also a companion. Four times a week, we embark on fifty minutes of intensely personal and emotional conversation, as she forces me to re-evaluate my response to life's challenges. I've confided in her secrets never spoken aloud before. She knows me better than anyone, much better than my mother does. She's another — in many ways far better — kind of mother: a clear-eyed ally, a sensible counsellor, an essential service. She's re-parenting me.

Friends and family don't understand. "Four times a week?!" they cry. It sounds so self-indulgent. Think of Woody Allen, on the couch for decades yet still a deeply flawed man. What was the point?

Not long ago, I was lying there talking to her about being a writer, my conviction that I'm inadequate, untalented, unworthy of the name. She listened gravely as I outlined my deficits. "Someone told me once I had the curse of 'surface brilliance,'" I went on. "I'm shallow and impatient, don't think or explore deeply enough, just want to get it done. I write fast. Good writers do not write fast."

There was a pause, and then her voice. "What's wrong with writing fast?"

As her words hit, I felt the top of my head explode. What's wrong with writing fast? Well, it's wrong because ... because that's how I do it.

In that moment, I realized how profoundly I handicap myself, how my lack of confidence undercuts me in every way. Rather than accepting that this is simply the way I do things and getting on with it, I paralyze myself with criticism and self-doubt.

What's wrong with writing fast? Nothing. Nothing at all.

It's as if the basement level of my psyche, my deepest self, was cluttered with fear, anxiety, negativity, self-hatred, and more bad stuff. I'd slammed that basement door, nailed it shut for years, to be able to cope with daily life. When the doctor and I began work, it felt like we were prying the door open, inch by inch. And then, when it had at last creaked open, we ventured down the stairs, step by slow, painful step.

Now we're walking about that subterranean space, shining a light into the murky corners and cleaning them out. We're inspecting what's there, bringing it up into the sun, throwing it into the garbage, or, occasionally, reshelving it because it's valuable.

This is work, one of my life's big jobs. Slowly coming to terms with my past, my parents and childhood, my marriage and choices, and, importantly, my ex's past too, is a gruelling slog, every session illuminating and tough. I can't help fighting her sometimes, to protect notions I've stored down there for many years. But day by day, she's helping me see other truths.

If we'd been meeting once a week, I'd have closed that door every time I walked out of her office, with a whole week ahead, seven days in the real world to navigate. But meeting so often, there's no point resealing my psyche, because we're going to resume the next day: tidying, sorting, explaining, clarifying, exploring. Hard, invaluable work.

She is a small woman sitting in a big chair in a tidy blue room. Her hair is yellowy-grey, frizzy, controlled. She wears good quality but unostentatious skirts, blouses, and jackets, sensible chunky heeled shoes, the occasional extravagant necklace. Her eyes are golden grey, I think, her voice soft and rather high. She writes down every word I say.

We've not spoken for six weeks because of the summer holidays. I'm looking forward to this meeting and will dress to please her, although what I wear is of interest to her only in what it says about how her client feels today. I can wear anything. I can say anything, and she will stay with me.

She will stay with me.

I wrote this fast.

GARDEN OF DELIGHT

'd always thought gardens were a bother. For years, my husband handled all the "yard work," as he called it. "I'll be out back taming nature," he'd say, before going out to cut the grass. Except for a petunia or two, that was the extent of gardening at our house. He tried to keep the edges neat, and I tried to ignore the whole thing. It was hard enough keeping the kids alive and the house livable without adding another great big room — filled with leaves and bugs and backbreaking work —to my chores.

But one day, the nature tamer didn't live here anymore. Suddenly, it was all mine, the long green expanse of yard work. Forget it, I decided; not enough hours in the day, no idea where to begin. I bought a book called *The Reluctant Gardener* and was reluctant to read it.

Into my back forty, just in time, strode Dorothy. Our gardens were perpendicular, hers a stone's throw across my next-door neighbour's unfenced yard from mine. When she opened her back gate and pushed into my meadow of weeds and underbrush, she had found her cause. What a canvas for her skill and enthusiasm! And a willing pupil there too, if a bit sluggish.

She'd been watching me. Dorothy, a brisk Englishwoman in her early sixties, had also been a single mother once, had coped alone with children, work, house, and garden. She'd been good at all of them, though.

"What's this dreadful thing?" she'd say, crouching on her haunches during her tour of inspection, pulling at some obnoxious weed. "Look, these are lovely, you must fertilize," she'd say, scrabbling to rescue some limp shoots. "The poor things won't survive without moo poo."

"Water!" she cried. "Water water water." I obediently began to weed and prune, bought fertilizer and a new hose, and watered. Order began to emerge; not Versailles, but there was hope.

Then she directed her fierce gaze upward to my trees, indicating which branches should be trimmed to let the sunlight in, and which trees should disappear entirely. "I like pretty trees," she said, "but not horrible, unnecessary weed trees," pointing a stern finger at an invasive, overgrown Manitoba maple. One strenuous sweaty afternoon, fuelled by Dorothy's certain approval, I cut down the maple with a handsaw. She exulted in the new light for my plants. Severe with pests like earwigs, squirrels, raccoons, and sun-stealing trees, she took joy in each tiny seedling. "Oh look," she gasped, kneeling suddenly, her nose an inch from the soil, "that datura has seeded itself. Isn't it brilliant?"

We got into the habit of strolling to the corner store, which had recently, with laudable timing, transformed its parking lot into a garden centre. She helped me choose practical perennials that might survive despite my ignorance and our climate. "Admire them all you want," she warned, as I swooned over the big blue delphiniums, "but they're impossible." If Dorothy couldn't raise them, there was no chance for me. But bit by bit, month by month, we planted clematis, lilies, astilbe, cosmos, wisteria, morning glory. Glorious.

Inevitably, as we sat after garden work, two single women and a bottle of wine under a canvas umbrella, our conversation turned to domestic matters. Fifteen years older than I, Dorothy had a lot to say about raising healthy children as well as plants. Her husband had left her for a younger, childless woman with a glamorous job. Dorothy had raised two young girls and twin boys, now adults who keep a close eye on their mother's well-being. She dotes on her two grandchildren. Because her own family was spread around, she adopted us as a nearby substitute — mother, children, and greenery.

Of course she had advice about my kids. "I don't worry about your daughter. She's a powerhouse, like you," she said, although "powerhouse" is the last word I'd have used for myself. Dorothy was concerned about my boy, that he was insecure and fearful and struggling. I wouldn't admit — couldn't admit — that she was right.

Last May she helped me plant a long row of tomato seedlings at the back where our gardens would have intersected if my long-suffering neighbour hadn't been in the way, and by late summer we had a rich harvest. "You've become a real gardener," she said, as we sat slicing tomatoes and drinking in the starbursts of purple and white clematis, the black-eyed Susans, hydrangea, nicotiana, sweet-scented phlox and lavender, the rhododendron she rescued from someone's garbage, the sunflowers, and wild sweet pea. I didn't leave the city at all that summer, mostly sat in the garden, and looked. Hard to believe my clumsy hands had something to do with such profusion.

But the autumn brought devastation for my friend and mentor. A decade-old romance — "my beloved," she called him, the love of her life — turned into heartbreak when he decided to move on. Her back began to give her such pain that she reluctantly submitted to an operation, which left her helpless for weeks and in more pain than before. Walking with a limp when she could walk at all and unable to bend down to garden, she realized she could no longer cope alone. In the winter, she and her married daughter sold their own homes and bought a big house together on the far side of town.

And now she's recovering from an operation on her lung, enduring further tests, awaiting the diagnosis for her future. All this from one summer to the next. When she found out she had cancer, she told me on the phone, she went out to rip dandelions from the lawn. "I think of them as a kind of cancer," she said, "and I thought, 'Right, I've got you lot!'"

For a long time, this spring, it was hard to garden without her. What was the point, without my friend's encouragement and expertise? But then she recovered enough to visit, inspect, and urge me on. We walked slowly to the corner store and up and down the fragrant aisles while she commented on each plant, and we chose a few. I began to weed and water. I even planted a tomato, only one. It's hard to relish the loveliness Dorothy inspired in my garden, while she is in pain, and afraid.

What's needed now is a buddleia. My friend loves buddleias because after the war, they sprouted miraculously out of bombed-out buildings in London, adding colour and delicate beauty to the rubble. She'd found one for me last year, and we planted it before she moved, but it didn't survive the winter.

I will plant a new buddleia in honour of Dorothy who, I pray, will go on teaching me about colour and beauty, about patience, and sunlight, and the hard work that is love.

MOTHER AND SON # I

I t's snowing heavily, Friday night after supper — a brief moment of peace in the house. The teenage girl is out, with her gaggle of friends. My eleven-year-old son is wrestling fitfully with the dog, and I am reading the paper, conscious that soon I'll have to deal with the pile of dirty dishes.

"I know what, Mum," cries my son. "Let's go out and have a snowball fight!"

Of all the things I would like to do right now — enjoy a full body massage, pour Paul Newman a glass of wine, go to bed while the servants clean up — having a snowball fight ranks just about at rock bottom. I begin the litany: I'm tired, the kitchen's a mess —

"Aw, come on, let's do it," he says. "Think of the memories. Just the two of us, a snowy night ... You'll be sorry if you don't."

He has cleverly played the guilt and remorse card, against which I'm helpless; besides, he's right. Making memories, saying yes at least sometimes, is part of my job. I get up and put on snow pants, boots, a down parka zipped to the neck, hat, scarf, gloves. He slips on a jacket, conceding to the snow only in changing to boots and grabbing my shrivelled leather gloves, ruined last year during a similar snowfall.

It's beautiful in the backyard. A layer of glistening snow coats the trees like the crust of marzipan on my mother's Christmas cake ... but I'm not left long in contemplation. A snowball smacks me, and war breaks out. This is not a fair fight. My opponent, at birth, could throw anything a hundred yards. To say I throw like a girl is an insult to girls; I have strong arms, but I cannot throw. So he joyfully thwacks me again and again, while I bend and pack another snowball and send it wobbling into the ozone. The dog leaps high, snatching my feeble missiles in mid-air and crunching them. Demolishing snowballs is one of his great skills.

Behind us, gold light streams out from our kitchen and the neighbours' kitchens. In front, the steady snowfall, the iced trees, the tall boy laughing, hurling snowballs for the dog, who whirls through the air to catch them. I think, eyes misting, *I can't believe it's me, in a Christmas card picture like this.*

House, good times, me keeping two children afloat. Unimaginable during my twenties. Unimaginable even a few years ago, after our lives were upended.

Although, God knows, the reality behind the pretty scene is far from perfect; there's lots that could get better around here. The boy and I have our problems. This handsome young man, so graceful and funny, has lost or broken a good number of his possessions and has a famously destructive temper. At school he's what is known as a "creative underachiever," at least, by me. Unfortunately, while the things he's not good at are obvious, the teachers seem unaware or unappreciative of his strengths. He just brought home a test on which he got 30 percent. In one of the assignments, a test of imagination, he was asked to continue eight tiny hints of line to make eight complete pictures. I thought my son's drawings, all different, were witty and moving; they made me laugh out loud. A spiky M became a series of heart monitors indicating "Lively. Not so lively. Dead."

The teacher wrote, "Backgrounds need colours. Labels in blue ink (pen). Satisfactory ideas."

I was effortlessly good in school. It's bewildering to live with a child who's simply not interested, to whom marks, tests, and homework are meaningless, and the latest daring skateboard move — an ollie, a kickflip — means everything. One of my housemates is a blonde-haired, blue-eyed alien, a male of our species who has, to me, incomprehensible needs and wishes. It's easy to decide exactly what gift to buy his sister, whereas my Christmas and birthday presents to him have often been way off-base — complicated toys I thought surely a boy would love, Lego boats and space stations, an elaborate trainset, a Playmobil castle with a million pieces, a little oven to bake gross insect creatures. These, for a boy who couldn't manage the intricacies of shoelaces till he was ten, but who was riding a two-wheeler, fast, at six, and who zipped out of sight the moment he strapped on his first inline skates. He recently stopped my heart when he careened down what looked like a perpendicular sheet of ice, upright, at the speed of sound, on a snowboard.

It's taken me a long time to begin to see, not the imaginary son who's much like his mother, but the very different boy who's actually there. I'm finally learning to accept who he is, and who he isn't. I accept the fact that just as I'm about to give away the never-used castle, he pounces on it and assembles its turrets for an elaborate diorama of invasion and slaughter between our army and the Orks. I accept the fact that he can eat a foot-long meatball sub at any time, but cannot manage more than two tablespoons of Rice Krispies in the morning. I accept the fact, hard as it is to believe, that he is as thoughtful and poetic, as vulnerable, as tender, as any of the girls I know.

How can I guide and protect him when I barely understand him?

The backyard snow fight is over; beast, boy, and mother are exhausted. Inside, he lights a fire and roasts a marshmallow or ten, fending off the dog, while I lie down to recuperate. He comes over and stretches his skinny child's body out beside me on the sofa. We hug. Soon, this bond will change forever. I stroke his hair.

"Just think," I say. "One day you'll be some lucky kid's father."

He looks at me with clear eleven-year-old eyes, his flushed cheeks perfectly soft.

"Stop. You're scaring me," he says, and holds me tight.

TRIUMPH OF SOLO WOMAN

A few days after my husband moved out, a kitchen drawer came apart in my hand. Of all the crises surrounding the beginning of my new life as Solo Woman, this was one of the most fraught: standing there with a piece of drawer in my hand, twist ties and garbage bags spilling onto the floor, and no idea what to do next. It hit me with full force that I was now not only a single mother but a single woman again — a woman no longer standing by her man. My marriage had its problems, but it also had its benefits, and one of those was that the man who'd so far shared this house knew what to do at times like these.

My childhood was interestingly deprived, Mr. Fix-it-wise. My father, after hearing two bars of classical music on the CBC, could name the composer and list obscure details about his life. He knew Latin declensions, the complete saga of the War of the Roses, and the quality of all the different vineyards of Burgundy. He knew everything except how to use a hammer, a screwdriver, or a wrench. If something broke in our house, we threw it out, or my dexterous mother did her best to repair it, or it was sent out for a Little Man to fix. My parents' marriage floated on a raft of hard-working Little Men who kept us going, while my father led anti-war protests and played chamber music.

My ex-husband comes from a long line of handymen. When he puts up a picture, he meticulously measures and levels, drills a hole, and inserts a plug. I, on the other hand, once forfeited the damage deposit on an apartment because in the spot where I'd tried to nail a rug to the wall, the landlord counted ninety-two holes. What did he expect? The rug wouldn't stay up, so I just kept hammering in nails until it did.

After marriage I continued to look at broken things and tools as the great mysteries of life. Even a plugged drain, even a wobbly table leg were left for my husband to fix. I ignored the workings of mechanical things, including the car, once driving it for so long without oil that the motor had to be rebuilt.

All this time I thought of myself as a feminist, holding up half the sky and all that, just not a very handy one.

So when a broken drawer and many other technical difficulties threatened to capsize me, without a husband to fix them, my first impulse was to find a Little Man. But Little Men are both elusive and expensive. Next I looked for friends with whom to barter: if you fix the drawer, I'll make you dinner or find you a coat at Goodwill. But friends too can be unreliable and costly. Why … the thought began to dawn … why couldn't I do it?

Because of a million more important things to do with my time and energy, that's why. But toilets kept getting plugged. Children kept getting hideous toys — Barbie desks and model trains, which had to be assembled by deciphering hieroglyphs or pidgin English printed on flimsy bits of paper. *Oh, go on*, I kept thinking, *just try it*. So I dug up some tools one day, and a handy woman friend showed me what they were for. I felt like Helen Keller as she pressed screwdrivers into my palm — they have names! Robertson, Phillips, the little square-headed one and the little star-shaped one have names!

And when screws are loose, there they are, just what you need. As other needs arose, other useful devices appeared, like duct tape, needle-nose pliers, and even the dreaded power drill.

Friends helped at first but soon left me on my own, unsticking windows and installing shelves and — the greatest test — assembling furniture from Ikea without throwing myself on the floor and howling with rage. One day I opened the latest Canadian Tire sale flyer which had become my favourite early morning reading, and there it was: a Stanley toolbox in flashy red and discreet grey, 50 percent off. I spent a happy afternoon putting in tools and taking them out, finding just the right arrangement.

Recently my ex came by to pick up the children, and I asked him to look at the barbecue, because gas is one of my great fears. When he requested pliers, I brought him my toolbox, which he looked at in disbelief. It was a moment, not of triumph, but of regret, as he opened the symbol of my new-found, hard-won, belated self-sufficiency. Then he showed me how to fix the barbecue.

He showed me, but you know, there are things I still won't touch, and that rusty old barbecue is one of them.

Postscripts for The Break:

Garden: *We no longer rip up dandelions, which are now considered important for bees and other pollinators. Dorothy would certainly have changed her botanical behaviour with the times, but she did not have that chance. She moved back home to England, to her twin sister Lizzie's rambling country house; her sickbed was placed so she could look out the window at Lizzie's dogs, trees, and flowers. She died in that bed. Lizzie planted and tends a mass of pink and white roses on Dorothy's grave, in the village churchyard.*

There's a picture of Dorothy's new garden on the wall in front of me, as I write. Her present to me, my own garden, is one of the great enchantments of my world. I think sometimes it has saved my life.

Triumph of Solo Woman: *For the truth about this delusional essay, see "Eulogy for Len Cunningham."*

These essays appeared in:

Garden of delight, *Globe and Mail*, 1997
Mother and son #1, *Globe and Mail*, 1997
Solo woman, *Divorce Magazine*, 1997

THE NEW REALITY

Why shouldn't you have the right to become who you are?

Wayson Choy

A great sorrow is a great experience – a life without it seems a pale colorless thing to me – but I cannot help feeling that a great joy is more to my liking.

Georgia O'Keeffe

AT THE FRENCH TABLE

I t wasn't clear I could pull it off. The plan was to take my kids to France, where we'd stay briefly with a cousin who very kindly resides in Paris, and then visit my best friend Lynn, her husband Denis, and their children in Provence. My youngsters would imbibe French culture and language, and I'd imbibe a little French wine, eat a lot of cheese, and relive the year my family spent in France when I, like my daughter now, was fourteen.

Miraculously, many things made this dream possible, especially my ex-husband's travel points. He and I had once visited France together; although as a reluctant traveller he didn't enjoy the experience much, he was glad now to help his children make the trip. And so, very early one morning in July, three bleary Canadians stumbled out into the Paris dawn. I was the one who wasn't carrying a skateboard and who looked happy to be there.

Introducing two normal North American children: Anna, fourteen, interested in telephones, soap operas, and Leonardo diCaprio, and Sam, eleven, crazy about skateboarding, TV, and Nintendo 64. They both wear skateboarder clothing many sizes too big; they live for *The Simpsons*, MuchMusic, and Taco Bell. How would they survive nearly a month in France? More to the point, how would I survive nearly a month in France with Bart Simpson and Mrs. Leonardo diCaprio?

Unbelievable — within a few hours of landing in Paris, they'd discovered a skateboard store with the same absurd clothing as in Toronto but at twice the price. Jet-lagged, we trailed off to the one historic shrine they really wanted to see — Jim Morrison's grave in Père Lachaise Cemetery, where they stood with an international crowd of kids gazing devotedly at a headstone plastered with roses, while a security guard in dark glasses gazed at them. All they noticed in Paris were young people just like themselves.

As we sat in the high-speed train from Paris to Avignon, France was flashing by outside the window — fields of sunflowers and lavender as we sailed into Provence, ancient villages of golden sunbaked stone. Across the aisle, my son, eyes shut, was listening to the Doors on his Walkman; my daughter was reading *Seventeen* magazine. I wanted to shout at them, "Look where we are, it's France, open your eyes!" But you cannot force a child to see. I was a child touring Europe once myself.

Lynn's newly built, sprawling stone house in a mountaintop village saved the day; we had a home away from home, where Anna and Sam gradually opened up to another way of life. Meals were the first test. In France, a summer lunch is a big event, lasting an hour and a half or more. We all sat on the terrace, beside the rosemary and lavender bushes, and ate and talked, and talked, and ate. My kids sat at table confronting a lot of conversation and unaccustomed food — ratatouille! chèvre! — with their own little glass of rosé, if they wanted. They were expected to dine and converse just like grown-ups. This was a shock; they're used to grabbing a pizza slice or burger and fries at lunch, and sometimes at supper too. Sam looked at the knife and fork as if they were weird instruments he'd have to learn how to play.

For me, there was huge pleasure in relearning the ancient rituals of the French table, like the order of service: hors d'oeuvres, main course, salad, followed by the pungent riches of the cheese tray, fruit, and dessert, accompanied always, of course, by a basket of bread. Watching my friend, I was reminded that the French shop almost daily for the freshest ingredients, local, and in season. And in this country, when you want coffee, you go to a café and sit at a table, often with friends, unlike at home, where you clutch a Styrofoam cup as you walk around.

Besides protracted meals, sightseeing was also an acquired skill for my offspring. Lynn's children have camped from Wales to Dubrovnik; they've seen hundreds of museums, churches, and art galleries. For my kids, who see a visit to the lively Ontario Science Centre as an enforced educational experience, visits to old buildings and monuments were impossible to disguise as fun.

"It's good for you," I told them. "So enjoy." They enjoyed one visit enormously — when we stopped to see the two-thousand-year-old Roman coliseum in Nîmes and were refused entry because the rock group ZZ Top was setting up inside. So instead, we went to a modern art gallery and to their favourite place for lunch, McDonald's, where, as you'd expect, French adults can accompany their *royal cheese* with a cold beer or an espresso.

At the start of my own adolescent trip through France, instead of letting me lie happily on my bed at home listening to the Beatles, my father insisted on dragging me into cold gloomy churches and boring chateaux. But there were great times too — the Eiffel Tower and Galeries Lafayette, the boys on the Riviera — and through the years the good things, and the beauty of France, won out in my memory. I hoped it would be the same for my kids.

Anna found a lifelong buddy in Lynn's daughter Jessica, who introduced her Canadian friend to the novel concept of wearing clothes that actually fit. Sam was annoyed he couldn't skateboard in the village because the streets were cobbled, but then he unearthed a year's supply of colourful French comic books. All of us enjoyed watching American TV programs dubbed into French, especially *Beverly Eels 90210*.

Back in Paris after nearly three weeks in Provence, my two companions were now curious travellers who didn't complain about hours walking or touring the Louvre. Anna fell in love with Notre-Dame Cathedral. Staring at the luminous stained-glass windows, she said softly, "If I ever decide to believe in God, it will be because of this place."

Sam, confronting his thousandth crucifixion, turned to me. "I guess Jesus was the thing back then, eh Mum," he said. After his thousandth nude, he complained that women in olden days didn't seem to own any clothes.

That evening, at dinner in a hundred-year-old French bistro, my children carefully ordered in French, discussed what we'd seen that day, and relished the meal. My father, who so adored France that he insisted thirty years ago on sharing his pleasure with me, would have loved to see his grandchildren in that bistro. But, as they in turn opened to the pleasures of this great country, I felt he was there.

Best of all, on our last night, we discovered a boulevard where French skateboarders careened up and down, along the scarred marble fountain and over the old gratings. Sam shyly joined them. Anna, checking out these interesting French boys, begged me to go stroll around the neighbourhood for a while. So I strolled.

At home, the design of our kitchen struck me for the first time as awkward, particularly a poorly located kitchen counter. The handyman came to remove it, and we shifted the dining table to a much more convenient spot for family meals.

I'd hoped my children would come back from our journey spouting in fluent French about the Mona Lisa. Instead, we all learned something simple: that the most important ritual of the day is setting the table, and sitting down, and listening to each other, and tasting what we eat.

CHRONICLES OF CHRISTMAS

As this time of togetherness approaches, I remember one Christmas, a long time ago. At the age of twenty-four, I moved across the country to Vancouver where I knew almost no one, and so found myself alone, on Christmas morning, cat-sitting in someone's apartment. The little box my mother had sent sat under the rubber tree in the living room. Opening it, slowly, was my festive activity for the day. Luckily, a colleague had invited me for Christmas dinner. Still, it was a long quiet December 25th.

In subsequent years, there were friends to help make an occasion of the day, and then, unexpectedly, there was a life's partner, someone to spend Christmas with forever and ever. And then, just as suddenly, we were expecting a baby. That year we joined my parents in Ottawa on Christmas Eve. With great ceremony, my father opened the bottle of 1958 Chateau Mouton Rothschild he'd stored in the cellar for just this occasion — to toast new life in the family.

The following Christmas, there was a busy seven-month-old in residence, and from then on, the holiday was buried under snowdrifts of paper, boxes, and ribbons. When the next baby came, a few years later, our Toronto home became the centre of the family. My parents flew east for the celebrations. Auntie Do drove down from Ottawa with my brother and two dozen freshly baked mince pies. After his wife died, my bereaved Uncle Edgar flew up from New York for his first visit ever, to be with us. The house was really full then — my husband and I, our children, my parents, all those other relatives — one year my in-laws too, from B.C. — and always, in memory of that lonely day in Vancouver, a few people who didn't have anywhere else to go. Homeless waifs, we called them — a fixture, a necessity at our festive table.

After the groaning excess of dinner, my mother would pound out carols on the piano. We'd stand around singing in the paper hats we'd pulled from Christmas crackers, the table behind us strewn with plates, bottles, tangerine skins, and nutshells. As he sang, my dad loved to offend with his own irreverent lyrics; "Deck your balls with cloves of garlic," was his favourite. Later, the children would settle down to read with him or do a puzzle with Grandma and Auntie Do. My job — making sure everyone was happy, especially the overexcited children, and keeping the house habitable and food on the table — was beyond exhausting, and there was always a familiar family tension bubbling under the cheer, ready to boil over.

But this, I felt, was what Christmas was really meant to be.

The summer my first-born turned six, my father was diagnosed with stomach cancer. That year, we flew to Edmonton for the holidays. Our plates at Christmas dinner were piled high, as usual. In front of him sat a small bowl of turkey broth, which he couldn't finish.

The next year was very hard. There was an unbearable silence at the centre of our gathering, though we were all aware of the irony of our grief — my Jewish father had never really liked Christmas. At least, the religious, manger part; he loved feasting and giving gifts. The rest of us mourned and drank a good bottle of wine in his honour. After that, my uncle, Dad's brother, decided he didn't want to travel at such a difficult time of year.

"If I'm ever in Toronto, though," he deadpanned, "I'll be sure to look you up."

One bleak September not long after, my husband and I separated. Though we struggled, in the end with some success, to communicate openly, each year there has been a painful tussle over the children at Christmas — who would be where, when, for what. My aunt announced she could no longer manage the journey to Toronto; she and her mince pies would stay at home. My brother bought a house and decided to stay at home too. I was grateful to our homeless waifs for filling out the table.

Last year was a celebration of another sort: the guests included my ex-husband and his latest girlfriend. It was good to see him at the head of the table again, carving the turkey in his yellow paper crown. This year, though, he's overloaded with work and can't come. My mum bought a condo in Florida, so she'll be staying south. On Christmas morning, it's just the kids and me.

They'll be leaving home in a few years. I wonder — will I end up once more alone, with a small present under a large plant? I don't think so. I hope these young people will keep coming back, if they can. They seem to feel there's only one place to wait for the feast — at home, even if the dog and I are the only ones here.

One day, our ranks will swell once more. Perhaps I'll marry again, who knows? The kids will find partners. Maybe one day they'll make their own joyful announcements, and with great ceremony I'll open the bottle of 1982

Côtes de Beaune-Villages, inherited from my father and stored in the cellar, to toast new life in the family. On Christmas Day, the children of my children will settle down to read and do puzzles with their grandma. That'll be me.

Once again, there'll be a big turkey and the best tablecloth covered with debris and bottles and chaos and carols and paper hats.

And always, homeless waifs on a solitary leg of their own journey, invited to join us at the ever-changing banquet table of life.

From the ebb and flow of my house to the ebb and flow of yours: Merry Christmas.

PUBLIC SCHOOL

Who knew saying goodbye to a school would be a wrenching experience? We're all feeling it, now the time has come. My kids have been part of the life of a small Toronto public school for seven years, from the September my daughter arrived for Grade 5, to this June, when her younger brother will walk out of Grade 8 to head for high school, more than a foot taller than the day he walked in.

It's an ordinary little round elementary and middle school at the centre of the city, filled with children whose families have come from all over the world to the most multicultural society on earth, or so they tell us. My son Sam has just made friends with a girl recently arrived from Africa, whose mother was a princess in her village there. His other friends are Chinese, Portuguese, Sri Lankan, Jamaican, even a Caucasian or two, like him.

Through the years, I marvelled that the home and school committee, a racially and economically diverse gathering of opinionated parents, ever got things done, but it did, and one parent, Bernadette, brought freshly baked cookies to every meeting. I saw the difference made by a good principal, the person who sets so much of a school's agenda, the hum of generosity or pettiness or disorder inside its walls. If the heart of a school is positive and vigilant, a child will flow through good and bad teachers, and prosper nonetheless.

Both my kids were lucky enough to spend a year in Room 202, where they encountered Marie Lardino, the kind of teacher — gifted, committed, born to the job — parents pray their children will meet. At the end of the school year, in all classrooms but one, the children were happily preparing to go home for the summer. In Room 202, both boys and girls were weeping. One boy cried, "I want to stay in this class where we get to feel like human beings!"

The most macho boy in the class, staring at the floor so his tears didn't show, was holding his "Enormous Effort Award," an award the teacher gave each child, citing areas of hardest work and improvement during the year. This boy's award was for "Developing a conscience."

One of those emotional children was my daughter Anna, who'd had such a stimulating year in Grade 6, she didn't want it to end. The following September Sam followed his sister into Room 202, now a Grade 4/5 and again a humming, purposeful workplace. One boy, previously such a behaviour problem that he was regularly sent home, became a class leader, emulated by the others. Silent, self-deprecating girls began to talk, though softly. And my son, whose world revolved around X-men cards and baseball, began to lecture me about the premier's cuts to the education budget; about what Nelson Mandela's election would mean to children in South Africa. This boy who hated sitting still with pencil in hand sat down to his homework without pressure or complaint.

"I have to do this properly," he said. "She expects it."

Once when I visited the classroom, Marie told me about the children she teaches from all cultural and economic backgrounds, who come to school hungry, cold, exhausted, hostile, hyperactive, self-destructive; children suffering from the effects of absent parents, hours of violent television, the shock of immigration and racism.

"I understand the parents' desire to see 'back to basics,'" she said with intensity. "Kids do need math, spelling, and science, and those things were neglected for a while. But some parents want to impose a limited vision of education taken from their own years at school twenty or thirty years ago, in a unilingual, uni cultural society with women in the kitchen. That world is gone; you have to provide the basics in the context of today.

"Sitting in rows memorizing is not the answer. I think this," she said, turning to her classroom, "is the answer." The youngsters around us were absorbed in their independent activities, consulting each other before coming to her. "These children are on task. They're learning, setting their own goals, evaluating their own efforts, and helping each other."

It was a heartening sight.

My kids and I all have memories of special times there. They remember basketball games, dances, enemies, and friends. For me, it's Family Music Night, when I made an enthusiastic debut in the art of karaoke — "Killing Me Softly," in the staff room — which luckily my offspring did not witness.

Together, the school and I weathered crisis after crisis: many emergency calls, a croaking voice complaining of a raging fever, sometimes legitimate, sometimes on math test day; the time my son drew graffiti all over the boy's washroom, but only in pencil; my daughter's regular visits to the principal, who was concerned she was taking her friends more seriously than her education, and he was right.

It had its problems, this school. Although there were other fine teachers besides Marie, who cared about the kids and teaching itself, there were those who'd done things the same way for decades and saw no reason to change; who proceeded, it seemed, with little concern for children's feelings. There were threats of violence; Anna was terrified by an older girl who offered to rip her face off for an imagined slight. The students regularly saw needles and condoms on the playground, sex workers loitering on the periphery — and it wasn't much of a playground in any case.

My two are not graduating — how to put this? — overburdened with classical learning. I hate to compare what they actually know with what my friend Lynn's children in France have covered in their rigorous education. Still, when Lynn, who's a teacher herself, visited recently, she told me how much she wishes her school had some of the innovations that are in place here: the learning centre and the resource room, the mentorship program, the problem-solvers program, the science and nature camp, the sex education, the anti-racism, anti-smoking, anti-homophobia, and anti-drug initiatives. My kids don't read Latin, but they do know a lot about diversity, flexibility, tolerance, and caution, how to cope with the complex, fast-changing world into which they will soon move.

Best of all were the end-of-year concerts. As we sat, crushed in the stuffy gym, straining to see children from kindergarten to Grade 8 sing, dance, and play instruments, I was always moved to patriotic pride. This is my country, this is Canada, these parents of every race and religion, focused on that sea of children — that multicoloured, shining sea.

Now there's only one more assembly to attend: the graduation of Sam's class. His male friends have unrecognizable deep voices and burly shoulders. The girls are all intrigue, hair gel, and giggles. Many of them have had a hard growing-up, parents divorced or broke or troubled, their own conflicts, some toying dangerously, now, with sex, and drugs of all kinds. One young friend has such a burdened soul, she tried not long ago to take her own life. A month later, she was back at school. She and the others are on the basketball, baseball, and volleyball teams, in the band and the choir. They practice their French, they play the saxophone, they work hard on their science projects for the yearly science fair.

This inner-city school has struggled through the government's and the school board's yearly policy switches. Right now, though, it's dealing with a truly hostile battering, a destructive cyclone of cuts and changes. The premier of Ontario, Mike Harris, has decided to take a sledgehammer to the education system. His cuts are so relentless, drastic, and devastating that the teachers have been forced regularly to go out on strike, in protest. Instead of being in school, the kids were often at Queen's Park, marching and demonstrating with their teachers and many hundreds of parents, including me.

And yet, even during its own upheavals, the school never failed to help my kids through bad times, making them feel protected and cared for. These days, though there are still a few brave green ribbons of protest fluttering from the trees, it feels as if it's the school itself that's at risk, in need of protection.

Sam has donated his two black gerbils to a Grade 5 class; children enjoy the company of creatures smaller and more dependent than they. In September, the gerbils will entertain ten-year-olds in the little round school, and the tall teenage boy who doesn't have time for them any more will push open the doors to the next stage of his life.

We would like to thank Mrs. Aleinikoff and Mr. Friberg, Miss Lardino, Mr. Milliken, Miss Klebanoff, Mr. Nicholson, Madame Alimi, Mr. Tom, Madame Sweetman, Ms. Cooney, Mr. Harding, Mr. Slobodian, Mr. Williams, Mr. Miwa, Mrs. Trainor, Miss DeFalco, Ms. Megill, Miss Nichol, and many others. Thank you, from all of us.

May you miraculously, despite all, prevail.

MOTHER AND SON #2

E very so often, I need to stand back and contemplate the young man I live with — my son Sam.

He's fifteen now, handsome, skinny, and tall, with a scrub of platinum hair, bleached by his sister a few weeks ago. By day, he enjoys passing the time in Grade 10 of the local high school, where he's doing fairly well. That's a major improvement over past years; my boy can't sit still, let alone make his brain follow a straight, logical line. Detail, concentration, fine motor skills are not his strength.

But gross motor skills are. When it comes to movement and reflex — basketball, baseball, skateboarding, snowboarding — he's a finely tuned action machine, a blur on the horizon. He can pitch and catch, he can swish, he can ollie and grind and kick-flip. Through all these energetic pastimes, I, his admiring mother, have stood on the sidelines and admired. But now, with this latest craze, he has to go it on his own.

He has bought his own gun and taken to shooting people — not with bullets, but with paintballs, which splatter oil and colour instead of blood. From one day to the next, he dropped boyhood toys and games and adopted a different kind of plaything, a different kind of play. After his first session of paintball, at a friend's birthday party, he came home ecstatic, his body pocked with little round bruises. I was horrified. When he wanted to play again and again, and then when he wanted to buy his own gun, I wouldn't hear of it. That's when he asked me to sit down for a talk.

"Mum," he said, with intensity, "you may not like it, but the fact is — I'm really good at this game, because I'm agile and fast. An old guy at the place couldn't believe I'd only played a few times. It feels great to be so good at something, and I'm going to go on playing it."

Which is how I ended up, last Saturday, driving him and his friend Marcel to the paintball palace on the edge of town. For months, with uncustomary single-mindedness, this boy saved his chore money; he sold his Nintendo, raided his bank account, and accumulated $300. I agreed to buy the safety equipment, another $80. Even there, in the bleak, chilly concrete bunker, amidst the racks of guns and the T-shirts adorned with distended musclemen and naked women, I tried to drag him back.

"This is so expensive, so ugly and violent," I exclaimed. "You don't really want to do this, do you?"

He didn't hear me. He and his friend were poring over the gun.

Sam and Marcel and the others — excited boys of all ages, a lone grey-haired man singing "Camelot" to himself, a few fathers, and one brave mother — pulled on the grey coveralls, the protective shield like an x-ray tunic, and the helmet, and loaded their guns. While they listened to the kid with the earrings lecture them about safety, I peered through the splattered windows at the war-scape on the other side: burned-out shacks, walls made of tires, free-standing trees to hide behind, everything covered in the yellow slime of the paint. Why would anyone want to enter that dirty, dark, cold place on this gloriously sunny afternoon? My son, looking like an astronaut headed for the Crusades, came over and kissed me goodbye, the plastic mouthpiece of his mask touching my cheek. And then he was gone, into the war zone.

In some countries, I thought, a boy his age would be carrying a real gun, into a real war. Not here in this placid country, thank God. But he seems to be preparing himself for combat anyway; for the struggle, perhaps, of becoming a man.

Five hours later he returned home, glowing with victory. He had never been hit, except by mistake, by his own team member. Using wiles and dodges, he had Captured the Flag, shooting all the others, all the adults. They'd awarded him hundreds of additional balls, the grand prize. Safely home, the warrior lay down his weapon and allowed himself to be served nourishment: a mountain of spaghetti, a bucket of milk, a box of Smarties.

Where does this skill lead, I wonder? To the army, or a life of crime? Will he be a spy, a real life James Bond? He adores James Bond. So do I — but only as fantasy, not the reality of danger, murderous criminals, evil women. Has anyone ever given a thought to 007's mother, how she must worry about her boy?

I hope James Bond goes home and visits her, once in a while.

CHILLING AND PUKING

As the single mother of an adolescent girl, I've come to understand there are two reasons childbirth hurts so much. First, because a woman's body has to make way for a small person to squeeze through. Second, so that parents subliminally associate this person with pain. This prepares them for the teenage years.

I remember the instant I fell in love with her, my newborn daughter, Anna. I was sitting in a rocking chair in the dark, singing "Bye baby bunting" to the soft, warm weight in my arms, when something simply folded in my gut, some resistance. It was my own young self, giving in. I was giving myself up for the next seventeen years. No, for the rest of my life.

Looking at my girl now, I feel wizened; she's as fresh and gorgeous and alive as a human creature can be. Just as my middle-aged body is in some ways shutting down, hers is bursting into bloom, like a lush peony.

But our last few years together have been brutal.

It began slowly in this house, the agony of adolescence, but as it began to roll over me like a tsunami I recalled all the articles I'd read about teens, the words like "sullen," "self-centred," "over-emotional." Since birth, my darling daughter had been cheerful, warm-hearted, and open, the kind of girl who'd rather talk than eat or sleep. She managed to squeeze homework and family into her busy social life.

Anna barreled into fourteen and fifteen, and then she was angry; I was angry; we fought a lot. The force of her struggle stunned me, and perhaps scared her too. Whoever that was, living in my daughter's room, I didn't like her much. Suddenly she was never off the phone, unable to stay in a room or a car without the radio blaring; she was sharp-tongued yet closed-mouthed, uninterested in anything besides friends and boy bands. It happened so fast it was bewildering.

One of the key words in her new vocabulary, one of the polite ones, was "chill." That's all they were doing when they got together, her friends, chilling — except for another, newly favoured activity, puking. She came home from parties now with puking stories — which of her friends had puked where and for how long. And then came the day she told her own puking story. She'd sampled every kind of alcohol available at a party, and there was a great deal. She told me calmly she'd chosen to try it all there, because the party was at a close friend's, an easy walk from home.

"Perhaps she's got it out of her system now," I said nervously to her father.

"Perhaps," he replied, just as nervously, both of us thinking back a few years.

The neighbourhood kids would slouch outside the front door, waiting for Anna to come out and chill. They'd all been in the house many times, only now their faces were blank, as if we'd never met; both boys and girls with piercings, or neon hair and tattoos, or pants so vast and shoes so wide or high that the clothes looked like circus costumes to me. Did my generation, in our bell bottoms and psychedelic prints, look simultaneously so absurd and so dangerously out of control to our parents? They all smoked, too, these kids, and I didn't know which was worse, the easily accessible cigarettes or the just-as-easily accessible illegal stuff.

After a death in the family, it was necessary for me to fly off one weekend. My son went to a friend's, but Anna wanted to stay at home. "It'll be fine, don't worry," she smiled. Her two best friends moved in to keep her company. So I went, calling to check at eleven on Saturday night, as prearranged. "Everything's fine," she trilled.

As I walked up the front steps on my Sunday return, however, nothing was fine. The front yard was a mess of cigarette butts and empty bottles. And so were the living room and the dining room and the kitchen. The chaos was indescribable. And this, apparently, was after the cleanup.

She'd invited "a few close friends" over on Saturday night, and "somehow" the word got out; neighbourhood kids had poured in, and she couldn't stop them. In the end, just before my phone call, she had telephoned the police. So, I later found out, did the neighbours.

"I love the police," she told me with tears in her eyes. "I was like hysterical trying to get those guys to leave. I didn't mean for this to happen, Mum."

The state of the house was one heartbreak, but then the next one dawned: things were missing. A lot of my jewelry; some of our sound equipment; every drop of alcohol in the house, including bottles of vintage wine left me by my father. I wept, and she wept, and then we cleaned up.

Did I ground her for weeks? Did I make her pay for the broken and missing things? The answer is no. I had and still have no idea how to deal with such a headstrong and fiercely rebellious child. Growing up, I was a good girl, meek, afraid of my parents and teachers. My first real rebellion against my parents' authority was liking the Beatles, for God's sake! Nothing in my background prepared me to deal with a daughter who rejects my rules and wants to fight me at every turn — about curfews, homework, chores, clothes, hair, noise, the mess in her room. Just about everything.

A few months after the disastrous party, I was forced to go away again. Anna assured me vigorously she'd learned her lesson; nothing would happen. And when I returned, nothing had happened, according to her. A group of her closest friends had merely lived at the house for the weekend, sleeping in my bed, butting cigarettes everywhere, removing or breaking a few things. It was around this time her school informed me she'd been skipping classes and was in danger of failing the term. When I spoke to her about this shocking news, she was rude and defiant, as if to blame the pain of growing up on me.

Things looked pretty black, around then.

After a few months of banning her friends from the house, I relented one afternoon and let my desperately social daughter invite in a few neighbour kids. It felt safe, because I was right there, monitoring. While I monitored in one room, one of her guests in another slipped my laptop computer under his jacket and vanished. Nobody, it turned out, knew his last name or where he lived.

So I made a ton of mistakes and learned a lot, way too late, about parenting teenagers. I'm relieved to report that right now, things are turning around, I think. My girl reluctantly agreed to see a counsellor and kept going for a while; sometimes we went together. She pulled herself together at school, sort of. The air has cleared between us, and we laugh together again, sometimes. She had a part-time job for a few months, where they said she was responsible, personable, and efficient. She gets up in the morning, usually.

My dear daughter is living here again, instead of a foul-mouthed, heedless stranger. Most of the time.

Some of the time.

A few days ago, we discovered something precious to me had been broken. She assured me neither she nor her friends had done it, and once again, I decided, against my better judgment, to believe her. My girl said,

"Mum, even though I didn't break it, I want to pay to have it repaired. You've had a hard time recently. I owe you."

It's commendable that she's showing responsibility. I will still give her the repair bill, no matter how big it is. Because she does owe me, big time.

She read this, by the way. "Mum, you let me off easy," she said.

And that, I'm pretty sure, is the problem.

EULOGY FOR LEN CUNNINGHAM

A while ago, I wrote an essay about myself as a capable, practical handywoman, fervently wanting to believe that delightful image. But it didn't last. How much of my brief time on planet earth did I want to spend with a wrench in my hand, trying to figure out how to use it? Very little, it turned out. My brain had limited power, and most of it was needed to focus on writing, or children, or my students. Not for the torment of assembling bookshelves or fixing toilets.

So room was made in the budget for a Little Man. And there, just in time, appeared Len. Dear Len saved my house countless times. This is what I said, years after we met, when asked to speak at his funeral.

Some years ago, my young children and I were walking down our street when we saw a man squatting on the sidewalk, doing something to a fence. We'd been living in Cabbagetown for a couple of years, and I'd noticed this scruffy, friendly man and his beat-up car. Something about his face made me stop.

"Excuse me," I said, "do you fix things?"

"I either fix things or I make 'em worse," he growled. I told him our house was built in 1887 and things were always breaking and I'd been looking for a handyman. He gave me his phone number.

Little did I know my whole life had just changed for the better; that this brilliant problem solver would enable my family to survive where we were. Without Len Cunningham, we would have had to move to a condo in Mississauga. Instead, we were able to stay in our decrepit, badly renovated, totally impractical, falling down house in Cabbagetown. Because Lenny could fix things.

Lenny fixed everything. There was not an inch of my house he didn't tackle at some point in our years of friendship. He received a frantic message from me every week, sometimes every day. Did my phone calls say, Len, come over, have a beer, watch how well the sump pump works? No, I only called in times of desperation and disaster. Len, help, my basement's filled with some horrible substance. Len, hurry, there's a skunk trapped in the window well, the front door won't open, the back door won't close, the kitchen ceiling is falling in the dinner. Eventually Lenny appeared and put everything right, and the old house was briefly functional once more.

As he worked, he talked about his other life, as an artist, traveller, industrial designer, and single father, about his kids and his birds. I admired his intelligence, creativity, and self-deprecating wit, his wide-ranging interests, enthusiasm for music, and great scores at garage sales, including a Mona Lisa painted by someone with more chutzpah than skill. He'd point to a step-stool or a post-box and say, "I designed that." Lenny's thick fingers could do such delicate work.

And let's face it, the rest of him was pretty wonderful too, including that sturdy beer belly of which he was so proud. Len was an attractive man, invaluable to the single women of Cabbagetown. After my marriage broke up, I joked that my husband had been replaced by a heating pad and Len Cunningham. He gave advice about all kinds of things — cars, insurance, furnaces — and was like a kind, funny godfather to my children. We talked honestly and personally about being divorced, being parents. He'd boast about Chloe's teaching or Davey's travels, and then complain that after their last visit, his stash of President's Choice frozen dinners had disappeared from the freezer. "Never have children," he'd grumble.

"Waste of time," I'd say.

"Bastards!" he'd say lovingly. "Bastards." Such a vivid word, when it came from him.

Mind you, he became more of a curmudgeon as time went on, especially about politics. We argued violently about the NDP's Jack Layton, for whom he had an irrational dislike. "Smarmy bastard," he'd say. And then we'd jump in his wreck of a car, he'd push aside some junk on his front seat, put on Nina Simone or Ray Charles, and off we'd go to Ikea or Home Depot to poke around happily in door handles and Billy bookshelves and floor stains.

We all have stories about the times Lenny saved the day. Here's only one of mine: One August, on the afternoon of a big birthday party for me, the kids and I were preparing a grand outdoor barbecue for fifty or so people when suddenly thick storm clouds rolled in. My deck and garden were wide open to the black skies. Lenny was urgently summoned, and he came right over.

We dug out a tarp, and stringing bungee cords from fences, trees, and eavestroughs, he rigged the tarp elegantly over the deck. Soon we sat drinking beer in the pelting rain, sheltered in the deep blue of Lenny's tarp. The storm was so violent that a branch fell on nearby hydro lines, the power went out, and fire trucks closed off the street, but it didn't matter. My guests, when they finally got through, were safe and dry on the deck.

Lenny came that night as a guest. He brought me a pile of things he thought a midlife woman would need, including a magnifying glass and a long plastic container for pills. The funny thing is that though they were a joke at the time, they're in use now.

How well he knew us. He knew about our love lives, our sex lives, our home lives. He saw the worst — the insides of our toilets and our closets, basements, fridges. He was in our homes as our marriages fell apart, along with the heating and the plumbing. He was right there. And we trusted him with our secrets. We trusted him because he loved us. And we loved him. A great affair was going on between Lenny and half of Cabbagetown, until it was cut short.

Sometimes it seems to me that men, and manliness, are being devalued in our western world, to our detriment. I honour and pay tribute to what manliness, at its best, can mean — the decency and hard work, the thoughtfulness and patience, skill and strength with which good men struggle to take care of the world.

And chief among those good men, in our small world of Cabbagetown, was Len Cunningham.

Postscripts for The New Reality:

At the French table: *Something else I realized while visiting my friends in Provence: a single mother dines with just her children, so, with two against one, youngsters take over the chat. From then on, I made a point of inviting guests for dinner as often as possible, so my kids could listen to all kinds of adult talk and participate in the discussion.*

Both my daughter and son are now skilled hosts who love to entertain and cook for others, so our trip to France had more positive and lasting effects than I ever anticipated.

Public school: *Until Donald Trump, I thought Mike Harris was just about as heedlessly, cruelly destructive as an elected leader could be, smashing education, healthcare, the very city of Toronto, and more. But now, there's a new gold standard for cruelty and destructiveness.*

These essays appeared in:

"At the French Table," *Fresh Air*, CBC, 1998
"Chronicles of Christmas," *Fresh Air*, CBC, 1998
Public School, *Globe and Mail*, 1998
Mother and Son #2, *Globe and Mail*, 1999
Chilling and Puking, *Globe and Mail*, 1999

COMMUNITY

To be a good writer you have to be a citizen.

Nadine Gordimer

VILLAGE SPIRIT

I went to an unusual party the other night, a big wingding at my local butcher shop. Terry and Doris Michelin and their son Mark, of St. Jamestown Steak and Chops, were marking their anniversary: twenty-five years on the main street of the village where I live. Terry thought about holding the party in a restaurant, or in the bar of the old hotel across the street, but the atmosphere in those places, he felt, wouldn't have been right. The only place to celebrate a quarter century of serving the community was right there in the store.

So we gathered, friends, neighbours, customers, on the sawdust-strewn floor, on one side or the other of the long refrigerator case that divides the narrow shop. The case, usually filled with chops and chickens, sausages and salami, now served as a very high, white bar. Some of us couldn't help remembering that on top of the counter, four years ago, was a petition in favour of capital punishment. Even those of us who couldn't sign understood why it was there.

Terry says he feels lucky to have chosen this small town for his business, but we know the luck is ours. He and Doris are renowned for the steadfast goodwill that emanates from the store along with T-bone steaks, fresh Ontario cheddar, and brown eggs. Between them, they seem to have learned the life story of everyone who drops in, from the boozy old-timer buying a few strips of bacon to the businesswoman who leaves her BMW running outside while she picks up her veal. There's a personal word for everyone, a hunk of kielbasa for children, a bone for dogs.

Terry, a handsome, sturdy man with thick white hair and a gleaming white grin, is an enthusiastic participant in a popular fundraiser for the nearby community centre, a fashion show starring local women as models. Terry and other main street merchants escort the gussied-up models down the runway. Last year, to the merriment of all, the men too wore gowns. Terry looked good in floor-length blue satin, although the moustache was wrong.

A private woman, steady and wise, Doris had a tough start in life; she was adopted in early childhood by a farming family that overworked and mistreated her. She moved out on her own at thirteen and grew up with a deep commitment to children. For ten years, after her marriage to Terry, she tended not only her own two boys but over one hundred foster children, mostly babies; she still receives grad pictures and thank you letters from youngsters who lived in the Michelin house. Her older son, Mark, started part-time at the butcher store at the age of ten. When the younger, Santo, followed, Doris came to work too.

Buying pork chops and ground beef there can be an unusually therapeutic experience. Unruffled and deliberate behind the counter, Doris listens, asks questions, and shares her insights with honesty and warmth. I felt her calm eyes watching me as I went through the turmoil of divorce. Later, I joked to her that by the time I'd recovered enough equilibrium to consider dating again, Mark, who'd divorced at exactly the same time as I, was remarried, with a baby.

"You did what you had to do," she said quietly, "to become who you have become. Who you are."

Imagine, just from my brief time in the shop, she saw that much change in me. Instead of paying for therapy, I could have stood in St. Jamestown Steak and Chops listening to Doris.

Humorous pictures of various fundraisers adorn the store. The whole back wall, however, is covered with photographs of a different kind. In the centre is a portrait of a freckle-faced boy with a shock of brown hair, the Michelins' younger son, Santo. One photo shows Santo beaming, the day he caught his first big fish. The other pictures are of boys who have been helped by the Santo Michelin Memorial Trust Fund. Santo was murdered four years ago, at the age of nineteen.

As we toasted the anniversary with glasses of Terry's homemade wine, all of us remembered that June day, the horror of learning what had happened to the Michelins, our disbelief. Santo, who'd driven up north in his beloved new red truck to go fishing with his friend Wes, had gone to the aid of two men who'd just rolled a Jeep. When they asked the boy for a drive to the highway, Santo took them. The men, local thugs with long criminal records, shot Santo, and Wes, for the truck.

A customer at the party reminisced *sotto voce* about coming to the store that afternoon. "I had a big order for a dinner," she said, "and they weren't paying attention. I got so impatient! Then I saw the sign they were putting up: 'Store Closed. Personal Tragedy.'" She closed her eyes. "I'll never forget Terry's face as long as I live."

The murderers were caught, tried, convicted. Terry and Doris sat in court through it all. Afterwards, Terry commented on the bravery of the police officers who'd been shot at while apprehending the killers; one officer had been badly wounded. "Those guys were hurt, and then they just had to go back to work. They're the ones I feel sorry for, to have to go on working with that memory."

The Michelins' customers provided what support they could: flowers, visits, listening, and for some, signing the petition. Money was collected to plant a tree in a nearby park, in memory of Santo. Terry gradually came back to life. "You can't just stay on the shelf," he says. Some of his energy goes into the scholarships he has set up in Santo's name, to send disadvantaged kids to hockey camp. He sponsors a "Most Improved Player" hockey trophy, and children's baseball and soccer teams as well.

Some feel Doris has never been the same. Mark disagrees. "It took a long time for all of us," he says softly. "But Mum believes in karma and life after death. Her spirituality helped her get over it." Rather than finding time to grieve, the family had to work harder after the murder, because Santo wasn't there to help. "We all pretty much kept on going," says Mark.

Christmas, Thanksgiving, Santo's birthday are especially hard for Doris. She did not come to this celebration. "She's with her main man," someone said, meaning Doris preferred to be home with her grandson, Mark's little boy. Mark, who has his mother's clear gaze, his father's smile, and his own whole-arm sleeve tattoos, will take over the store one day.

The party wound down. Those of us who weren't ready to leave crowded into the office space at the back. We hailed the late arrival of our mayor and her husband, who live nearby; she stood beside a block of enormous knives, reminiscing about the days when she couldn't afford much meat. We laughed a lot. As friends, as a community, we were trying, in whatever small way, to help heal something that could never be healed, but that could, perhaps, be survived.

The village where I live is called Cabbagetown. It comprises a few thousand well-assorted souls of all incomes, languages, faiths, and colours, and it's located right in the heart of downtown Toronto.

"This is a real neighbourhood, where people look out for each other," Terry said, as we put on our coats. He held the door open for us, and we hugged him, and walked home.

— 45 —

RADIOHEAD

I miss him already. Until his recent permanent retirement, Peter Gzowski always came back, even after long absences, to his hugely popular CBC radio program *Morningside*. Every weekday his voice floated out over the airwaves to claim us, like a ribbon held by a teacher leading school children on an excursion. We listeners were all holding on to the coast-to-coast ribbon of Peter Gzowski's voice.

Yet for me, there were many Gzowski-free years — when I was studying, or at work early, or working at night and sleeping in. People around me were discussing various interviews and issues from the show, but I wasn't listening.

Then came the years when his program was a lifeline. From the high-charged stimulation of my acting work, I moved into the domestic cocoon of a stay-at-home mother of two small children. It's a hard transition from one kind of satisfaction to another, and although I was exactly where I wanted to be, there were days when the isolation inside the walls of the house made me nutty. But I never felt alone, because an intelligent, courteous man spent the whole morning talking to me.

By noon I'd managed to accomplish a few things perhaps, getting myself and children dressed and fed, a load of laundry or dishes, picking up toys, all while absorbed in interesting, sometimes unforgettable, conversation.

I was working in the kitchen the morning Peter interviewed a soft-voiced Prairie woman who'd just put out a book of poetry. Her name was Elly Danica. The book, called *Don't: A Woman's Word*, was about her nightmare childhood during which, she told us, she was sexually abused, for years, by her father and his friends. This was before adults had started to speak publicly about the secret horrors of childhood. I had to stop and sit down, to be able to comprehend what she was saying. My mind kept repeating, *Her father? And his friends?*

As her steady voice told its tale, I was so devastated I could hardly move, and wondered whether everyone listening across the country was as heartsick.

It felt like all of Canada uncovering the reality of child sexual abuse right then, all together.

And then there was the rollicking interview with the couple who'd been surprised with a pregnancy when the wife was forty-nine. Holding their one-year-old whom they'd brought with them, they talked about getting all the baby things they'd bought for their grandchildren back for their own offspring, about facing old age and mortality with a young child. The baby started to babble into the microphone, and the grown-ups shut up to listen. From the stillness of the studio came a long series of musical gurgles, a much-loved baby singing his song. Peter laughed. "Hundreds of thousands of Canadians," he said, "are listening to baby talk."

With Gzowski, even listening to baby talk, I wasn't simply one of countless Canadian housewives listening in her kitchen, I was a citizen of a vast country of fascinating, brave, quirky, opinionated, hilarious, literate, talented, world-travelling citizens. Through the years, though he doesn't know it, Gzowski interviewed me, too — about my scintillating life, my fabulous children, my hopes for the future.

He wasn't perfect. Sometimes he was gruff, sometimes unctuous, too ready to please; points that were important but perhaps not pleasant slipped by. Or he was too polite to detestable people, or not polite enough to admirable people. Yet during all his years at the microphone, I never heard him make a single major gaffe.

What is it that made him special, that makes his replacements, charming as they are, not quite … Peter? They're so much younger, for one thing; they've experienced so much less. Peter has been there, done that. He was relaxed, warm, and open, his humour self-deprecating and generous; he made his guests comfortably welcome while probing their lives. His style, the same with heads of state as with village bird watchers, was intimate, down-home, as if all those strangers, one after another, came to sit in his kitchen while he poured coffee and sliced his special banana bread.

Yet for all his seeming effortlessness, he was a superb craftsman, alert and well-prepared; he shaped interviews, bringing people back to missed topics, picking up loose ends. He even managed an ending for most of the talks, a wrap-up flourish or a laugh line. In the U.S., this would need to be a big moment, because the prime concern of the network is selling the advertising space that follows. Here, Peter's finales led to a nice piece of music, and then Peter again, more coffee, more banana bread.

How reassuringly Canadian, that this far-flung population was united by a single radio personality, like the CPR. And what a Canadian personality. Not a raging right-wing blowhard, like those popular on the radio south of us, or a man of any political stripe whatsoever — in fact, what are Gzowski's politics? Who is Peter Gzowski, anyway? We know his clothes are rumpled, he wasn't a hit on TV, he plays golf and smokes a lot. Otherwise, when you consider the man is as ubiquitous as any Canadian politician or entertainer, we know remarkably little about him.

I see Peter as the ideal small-town barber. You sit in his chair and jabber away, and he listens and asks questions, and you talk some more. And at the end, he whips off the cape, you look in the mirror, and you're the same person, only better — sharper, funnier, more knowledgeable, more in touch.

Come back to us, Peter. Let us sit in your chair while you make us look better, while you make us look at each other. How can we join this country in the morning, from sea to shining sea, without you?

RUNNING

J ust after my fortieth birthday, life changed drastically for me. My marriage ended, and a different career tentatively began. As a newly single mother and beginning freelance writer, I felt doubly alone. There was nobody to talk to at work during the day, and nobody my own size in the evening either. It was a lonely, frightening time.

So I went to the Y.

I'd always been a casual member, some aerobics here and there, months of prenatal exercise classes. But now I started to go to the lunchtime run-fit sessions, partly to break up my silent work day, and partly because a couple of the men who attended those particular classes on their lunch hours were acquaintances of mine.

Let's face it, I joined the run-fit classes to meet men.

Not to go out with men — the last thing my life could fit in just then was a new relationship — but for male companionship. As a divorced woman, I was instantly cut off from an important chunk of my former social life. Married friends didn't invite me over any more as they had when I was half a twosome. Why? I wondered. Untethered to a partner, was I a threat? Boring? Embarrassing? Pathetic? Dinner parties vanished overnight; a solo female just doesn't fit around a table neatly laid out for couples. My women friends were there as always, supportive and loving, but I was completely cut off from the company of men.

Except at the Y. The same guys kept appearing at the classes, and we started to talk. It took months, years of running around in circles before real friendships sprang up. But gradually, I made some good friends. And while that happened, almost without paying attention, I was running.

I ran at the very end of the line, with the slowest of the slow, for a long time. Sports had never been my thing. I was disqualified from a school swimming race once for walking instead of swimming through the shallow end to the finish line. God help me, growing up it was my fate to be tall and good at school; if I'd been sporty too, I'd never have a boyfriend. Most girls didn't do sports then anyway. Females weren't supposed to sweat, or compete. My only sport was ping-pong.

I did have a flash once, playing basketball in gym class at twelve, dodging and passing and charging after the ball. As my body raced, lithe and strong, sheer joy blazed through me. I thought, as I ran, *I LOVE this*!

And then that thought was locked away in my mental bottom drawer along with my wish to be a ballerina, and beautiful. Forget it. Not for you.

When that surge of sporty joy hit me again at forty, it was not through interest in fitness but through need for friendship. Then I began to feel it regularly, because I started to attend the classes regularly — twice, then sometimes three times a week. I got to know all the teachers, who had the best routines and tapes. One of the other women and I began to discuss our healthy addiction to the place and became confidantes, so much so that one exciting day, we actually met, fully clothed, outside the Y. It was a first.

As I struggled day to day at home, my pals in class became a cheering section, not just for my fitness level, but for my life and work, as I was for theirs. "You were dragging today, you okay?" one would ask, or, "Any luck with that job?" There were times, many times, when the only adults who knew what was happening in my life were my buddies at the Y. I developed a big crush on one class member, a nice guy who was a safe choice because he was happily married. I could appreciate him without worrying about the dangerous possibility of something actually happening between us. Seeing this good man regularly kept my heart alive.

One day, sitting on a rowing machine, I caught a glimpse of my sturdy legs in the mirror and flashed on a memory of my father's thin limbs. He'd nearly died of polio when I was a year old, and although he regained mobility, some of his muscles had been forever damaged. Nothing showed, nothing stopped his energy and charisma, and we never, ever spoke of disability, but there were things he could not do. We never skied as a family, because he could no longer ski. He couldn't run.

Staring at my brand-new muscles, I realized my drive to fitness had not begun until shortly after Dad's death. And a startling revelation about my decades-long aversion to sport left me stunned and motionless. *Is it possible,* I asked myself, *I never before ran or played any vigorous sport, despite having an athletic body, because I didn't want to do anything my father could not do?*

How else to explain the radical change in my habits and behaviour? But whatever the reason, my resistance to sporting activity, to moving this body, was gone.

My running got better. I started to keep pace in the middle of the pack, where if you slow down, you get trampled. Doing my first 5k race at 10am one New Year's Day, I marvelled that instead of moping around, hungover, I was loping down Yonge Street. A job even came my way through Y connections, when a friend in the ad business hired me to help him with a big writing project. Our partnership was a success. We knew each other's strengths and weaknesses well after years of running around together.

Has any of that running around ever gone further, you ask? Even though most of my Y buddies are married and fathers, strictly out of bounds, still, there we are, damp, breathing heavily, wearing skin-tight bits of nothing. But no, I enjoy the best of those guys, right there in the gym. What if I went out with one and we broke up? Who'd get custody of the class?

These days, my sorties to the Y are still among the most important touchstones of my week. I follow the instructor blindly, like a duckling, and chat and muse and watch the other runners — the ones who are heavy and weighed down, the ones who are light and loose or stiff or gangly or buoyant or sleek. When the class ends, I'm tired without even noticing how I got that way. All this comes as a gift while I am running running running at the front of the line.

Now I'm one of the sweaty, competitive women I used to watch from the back, speeding along just behind the fast ones. Very sweaty; almost competitive. It's me, headed for fifty. I intend to hit that fine decade moving, and talking. And the same for every decade that remains to me while I still have breath in my body, and two functional knees.

Yes, I think as I hit my stride. *I LOVE this.*

BABY JESUS COMES TO CABBAGETOWN

One January afternoon, my friend Mary and I were strolling through our neighbourhood, Cabbagetown, talking about the Christmas pageant. Mary's church, St. Peter's Anglican on Carlton Street, used to produce a pageant every Christmas Eve at nearby Riverdale Farm, with local churchgoers playing wise men and shepherds, and at the end, a family with a real baby sitting in the straw of the barn. The farm's animals loitered in their stalls on the periphery, snorting out icy December steam.

But the minister who loved singing and theatrics had recently moved away, and the new minister wasn't interested in producing anything except sermons. There'd been no pageant that past December. We mourned the loss, Mary as a church-going Christian, and I as an atheist whose children often spent Christmas Eve with their father. Going to the farm was a joyful way to spend a solitary evening, moving with the crowd, singing the grand old carols from my childhood that always made me cry. "O Little Town..." "Silent Night." "It Came Upon a Midnight Clear" — tears dripped down my frozen cheeks as I sang.

Now the pageant would be no more. Until Mary turned to me and said, "This coming December, why don't we do it?" And I looked at Mary and said, "Well — why not?" How hard could it be? Get a bunch of people to act the parts, tell our friends, et voilà. Right then, like Judy Garland and Mickey Rooney, we decided to put on a show in a barn.

Surely there's no metropolis anywhere else in the world with a seven-acre farm smack in the middle of downtown. Cabbagetown has been my home for years, and Riverdale Farm is one of the main reasons it's hard to imagine living anywhere else. The farm, run by the city, is free and open 365 days a year, and not much happens there. It's not a petting zoo. Mostly, when you visit, you get to smell farm animals and watch them chew, and nothing, in the middle of a crazy city day, is more restful and reassuring than that.

I undertook the writing of our pageant script, a masterpiece of simplicity designed for an amateur cast, with one stirring line for each actor, like,

"Look, the star!" As I wrote, I wrestled with the ghost of my father. Dad hated anything that smacked of organized religion and thought people who believed in God were brainwashed fools, with the exception of Albert Schweitzer. So as I wrote the line to be spoken by Wise Man #3, "We are searching for a baby, the son of God, the prince of peace," Dad was snickering at my elbow.

Mary and I cast anyone we could drag in, mostly our children and friends, and importantly, a couple with a baby. A seamstress neighbour turned bits of material into cloaks and headdresses; the other costumes we fashioned out of bathrobes and sashes, with tea towel headgear for the Wise Men. For the final tableau in the barn, we bought angel wings for the little ones who'd stand in the manger, and for the baby's mother, a length of bright blue sari silk from Goodwill to drape around her winter coat.

It was hard to pull the busy cast together to rehearse their line. So on opening night, which was also closing night, the co-producer, playwright, director, and stage manager — me — hadn't even met some of them. And yet at 7 p.m. there they all were, in costume, with almost two hundred people waiting in the cold. And so it began.

Our biggest challenge each autumn is to find a baby with parents willing to spend Christmas Eve sitting in an unheated barn. Our first year's baby boy was so perfect a few people around here still call him Jesus, though his name is Wylie and he's now five.

That year, it was 18 below and snowing, and the carols we'd printed in the program went on for so long as our teeth chattered that I ended up shouting, "Cut to the last verse!" on every one. We redid the songbooks after that. A woman said as she left that the show was nice but someone should inform the cast that angels don't chew gum.

Our second year's holy family decided not to sit on the fresh bales of straw put in the manger stall by farm staff, but instead dragged in a bench. It just looked odd, the holy family in the manger, perched side by side on a bench. As baby Jesus began to howl, an old man turned to me with a beatific smile and said, "At least in one place, it feels like a real Christmas." And then he realized the goat in the stall behind him was nibbling on his jacket.

The third year a young shepherd forgot her line and stood frozen while the narrator prompted, "Perhaps there's a baby? A star? Leading you to the baby?" The second Wise Man, eighteen-year-old Jesse, ran over at the last minute from his job at the local beer store, put on his cloak and tea towel, climbed up on the picnic table with the two others to say his line, and ran back to work. The third Wise Man, another local boy — one closely related, in fact, to me — amused himself by making farting noises in the manger, and Joseph kept turning around to frown. My boy, at six foot three, looked strange with his huge Nike's sticking way out from under his brown velveteen cloak. As the years go by, our sons have become increasingly resistant to doing it again.

Every year we have trouble finding Wise Men — something our pageant, and the world, have in common.

My daughter tells everyone she's the star, which she is; she walks ahead of the crowd holding a long pole topped with a bamboo star draped in Xmas lights. When the shepherds cry, "Look, the star!" she flips a switch and the lights sparkle. The magic of special effects.

Last year, when the pageant was over and we were packing up costumes and props, Hakim the head farmer told us Matilda had just given birth. While we were celebrating a nativity in one barn, Matilda, a big black sow with ears like blinkers over her eyes, was producing her own in another. Hakim allowed us to peer through the pig barn window, to admire five bouncing Christmas piglets with ears like blinkers.

Every year, a new laugh, a new mishap. Local people are devoted to the event, though it has grown so, over the years, the size of the crowd has become a problem; some complain they can't see, and they can't hear. They say it goes too fast, or, when it's really cold out, it goes too slowly. We dream of proper outdoor lights and a sound system. Mary longs for a real camel. There was talk once of our farm being affiliated with the huge city zoo, and we thought, *Well, at least we'll have our camel.*

What matters is that we all end up in the barn with the shaggy majestic Clydesdale horses and Dusty the donkey, the cows, goats, and sheep, and the family with their child, surrounded by tiny solemn angels with tinsel halos and big white wings. There, in the sweet tang of animals and straw, the crowd sings "Silent Night," and every year, exhausted and elated, I cry.

Friends have asked why I of all people am involved with this event. They know I don't believe in God or in the divinity of a Jewish prophet named Jesus. I just love those old carols, is my explanation, and the hokey simplicity of our neighbourhood production.

But also ... I regret I don't have a formal, organized belief system to pass on to my children. I wish I could give them a creed, faith in something bigger than they are, something solid and sustaining to turn to, especially in times of grief and pain.

But perhaps I have. I believe in the power and the glory of the newly born, whether with round pink noses or snuffling bristly ones. I believe with all my being in neighbourhood; in ritual and community; in coming together at important times, to sing in celebration.

And, because of our yearly communal event, I think my children believe in those things too.

GOODWILL JUNKIE

W hat kind of person threw that away? The question is always running through my mind. Who threw away the brand-new Irish knit sweater? The piece of hand-carved Quebeçois folk art, a logging wagon drawn by horses with perfect miniature harnesses? The quilted Chanel handbag? I know the answer to that one, because she left an unused cheque in the inside pocket. Whoever you are, Marsha T., you are my friend.

In fact, these generous people did not throw these items away; they gave them to Goodwill, and that's where I found them. Second-hand shopping is not only my hobby, it's one of my most valued skills. I'm famous not for my fragrant baking or fragrant bouquets from my garden, but for my unfragrant gifts from Goodwill. I like to give people coats. "You didn't get this …?" they gasp, as they slip on my bulky offering. That question makes me laugh. Do they think someone with my income would go to The Bay and simply buy them a coat? Think, people — I'm a writer!

The answer is: trolling the aisles of my local Goodwill, as I do regularly, I spotted an interesting fabric, colour, or shape and thought, that tiny coat would look great on Gina, who's a size 4. That one would look great on Wayson, on Patsy, Denis, Annie, on Mum or Auntie Do. And much of the time, it does.

In 1968 in Ottawa, my first long-term boyfriend took me to Crippled Civilians, as the junk stores, unimaginably, were then called. "Mousie," he said, which is what my eighteen-year-old self, unimaginably, was then called, "I want to buy you a mink coat," and he pointed to a long rack of thick brown minks, glossy sheared beaver, mouton. Each cost $5. I was horrified. How could he bring me to this shabby place smelling of other people's sweat? What kind of guy would want his girl to wear something a stranger had worn and discarded? The answer: a guy whose favourite tie had a German shepherd painted on it. When I needed a new desk, the prescient boyfriend suggested we go to a second-hand store and find an antique roll-top. Why buy something so bulky and old? I bought plain teak, new.

A few years later, a poor student then actress, I began of necessity to drop in to Crippled Civilians. To my surprise, there was interesting stuff. My first ever purchase was a hand-knitted sweater, the name "George Armstrong" sewn inside, with a colourful hunting scene on both front and back, an elusive fox on the sleeves. I scolded George for giving away something made for him with such effort and skill and wore that sweater — which Ralph Lauren must have seen because he made countless lesser copies — for three decades, until it surrendered to moths. A boyfriend commandeered it once, but when we broke up he was required to give it back.

My outfit at the twenty-first birthday dinner my parents held for me in their backyard was a beige silk flapper dress bought on Portobello Road in London, with rips and stains I fondly imagined were part of its charm. My American grandfather, Pop, flew in from Florida for the event. He'd made his living in the dress business and disliked his granddaughter wearing second-hand, he who'd had to wear hand-me-downs as a child and fought all his life for the respectability of the brand-new. As a birthday gift he wanted to buy me a pantsuit made of his favourite new miracle fabric, no-ironing-required polyester. I requested a portable electric typewriter.

A feverish bout of respectability hit me at thirty, with marriage and babies. My grandfather died contented; finally, his hippie polyester-deprived granddaughter was safely stowed, no more second-hand for her. Except for baby stuff — cribs, highchairs, prams; how wasteful to buy those new when they'd be used for such a short time. My husband and I drove for nearly an hour to find a crib advertised in the *Buy and Sell*. As soon as we got it home, the slats fell out of the sides, and we tied them back in with string.

When we landed in Toronto, there were fancy social functions to attend. In search of some affordable dressy clothes, I discovered resale designer boutiques, like palatial Goodwills where the second-hand stuff is more expensive but clean. And then came the divorce, with its requisite huge reduction in income, my limited resources further drained by the cost of therapy. One winter day I needed a sweater and for the first time walked into the Goodwill on the main street of my neighbourhood. I'd passed it many times, sure that my dignified, mature self had outgrown that eccentric phase. Now here I was back in the musty store smelling of other people's sweat. And there I have remained.

That day a Missoni sweater in perfect condition leapt out at me. Seeing the label made me freeze, then hyperventilate. I bought it for $3, rushed home breathless with joy, tried it on, decided it didn't suit me, and took it back for a refund. Returning a Missoni sweater to get your $3 back is what's known as a mistake. But a new kind of shopper was launched. The riches in that chaotic mishmash of a store floored me, like the antique quilt, a little torn, tossed onto a pile of junk. The lady at the cash snorted at the rips and charged one dollar. There were jackets, handbags, rugs, heavy coffee table art books. There was an entire toy Western village from the fifties, cowboys, horses, buffalo, props — little campfires, headdresses, teepees, bags of gold. My children looked at me strangely; what would we do with an entire miniature Western village? Especially when I wouldn't let them play with it because it might be worth a lot of money. (It was not.)

This is a true addiction, because I hide it. "Just going to do some errands," I say cheerily, as if it's necessary to go out every day to buy stamps and moisturizer. But really, I'm off to my strange place of pleasure and pain.

In my version of hunting and fishing, I go in hoping to hook something wonderful: a sturdy chair for the backyard, a Harrod's apron, a pair of vintage sunglasses, a new bestseller — something unique, perhaps nutty, perhaps beautiful. My deal with myself is to get in and out as quickly as possible, starting with a figure eight around the racks — dishware, bedspreads, books, always the books. And then making my way slowly along the coat rack, all senses focused, spinning — eyes, ears, fingers, moving in all directions, seeking that spark, trying to spot quality.

One of the first things I learned the hard way is that almost always, there's a good reason something has landed here. Sometimes it's damaged, more often it's hideous; even the great couture designers have made some dreadful mistakes. But their names — Chanel, Dior, Pierre Cardin — and some label names — Mondi, Max Mara, Missoni — still make my knees go weak. Unfortunately, the staff now recognize those names too, so stuff of real value appears more rarely. And now, rather than giving their stuff to charity, rich people often take it to resale stores.

Buying second-hand has become trendy. Through the years I thought of all of us in the store as weird junk-store junkies, but now nice normal people are making this addiction their own. The place has filled with aggressive dealers, and the regulars complain it's hardly worth going any more. Still, I've managed, year after year, to find a few treasures and haul them home.

The big problem is, if the stuff isn't given away, it has to go somewhere. Through time, my bedroom, kitchen, closets, and then the basement began to fill with a rising tide of junk. Besides the random items, there are my official collections: afghans and quilts; antique English dishes; wooden toys, pull toys, old toys of all kinds; books old and new; lengths of sari silk; vases; baskets, briefcases, and bags; framed pictures; puffy white satin wedding albums that break my heart. (What kind of person threw that away?)

And of course clothing, especially vintage: sixties gowns my grandfather would have loved in glittery stretchy polyester, beaded sweaters, sleek forties dressing-gowns with shoulder pads. I finally got my fur coat, then two, then three. I owned four embroidered Inuit parkas until one was given to a neighbour and two to an auction fundraiser at my son's school. The school was also happy to sell the tall pile of *Hardy Boys* books, collected one by one, dating from 1946. Friends started to lecture me about clutter. Clutter? This was treasure, treasure that was mine, all mine!

My fantasy was that the collections were worth a lot of money; that apart from clothing myself, friends, and extended family cheaply, I was actually accumulating capital. "If a bus hits me," I'd say to my kids, "call Peter the antique dealer." On entering my stuffed home, Peter would surely offer a fortune for my astounding trove. My unbusiness-like self did try, several times, to deal with the accumulation in a business-like way. At a designer resale store I pretended to be a wealthy shopper bringing my own expensive clothing to sell on consignment, including Prada boots, a Gucci T-shirt, even a rare, very valuable Pucci top. Pucci! When, some months later, I tried to collect on what I'd left there, the store owner who'd pretended to be honest said she hadn't been able to sell anything and had given it all away.

Next a friendly dealer came to my home to view the mountains of stuff. She took six full garbage bags and many hangers of clothing and paid me $375, which didn't remotely cover the expense of buying and cleaning it all. Because let's not forget the dry-cleaning bills, or that the fee for repairing the one-dollar quilt was $150. There's a cost to this kind of shopping.

Not to mention the time it consumes. Each item the dealer threw into those garbage bags had been seized, inspected, mulled over, paid for, taken home, inspected, mulled over, admired, and finally put up for sale. The number of hours that has gone into my cheap hobby is unthinkable. If you factor in my time, those cheap finds cost far more than at Holt Renfrew.

But without the thrill, the game, the pleasure of noticing, pouncing on, rescuing, and cherishing a unique item that would otherwise be discarded. A woman who owns an actual vintage store — where I don't shop, because what's the fun in that? — introduced me to a friend as "one of the great amateur pickers." That made me beam with pride, even if my grandfather would not agree. It's a world unto itself, the ecosystem of Goodwill, where all manner of people hang out. Some of them are disconcertingly odd, it's true, and I wonder why the only normal one there is me.

Just between us, sometimes the place feels like my sex life. Finding a gem buried in the dust is the equivalent of an orgasm. "Oh my God," and a moan escapes my lips. "An Italian leather briefcase." "A framed Kandinsky print." "A floor-length pleated polyester evening skirt." Touch it, hold it, bring it home, and fondle it again: a banquet of sensory indulgence.

There's the enormous gratification of giving something of real worth to others. When my adored uncle in New York was diagnosed with cancer and very sick, I visited regularly to help care for him. He was a man of means; what could his impoverished niece offer? One winter I appeared with a long down Ralph Lauren coat, just his size. He needed down, now that he was so frail. That perfect coat kept him warm for two years, until he didn't need it anymore.

Because many people shop at Goodwill out of greater necessity than I, I make sure my purchases are rarely anything that might be of value to a family in need. Besides orgasms and gifts, there's another good reason to shop this way. I despise the fashion magazines' "Must Have" section. Who are those anorexic sticks to tell us what we must have? Conspicuous consumption is not only obscene but boring; anyone can walk into Holt Renfrew with thousands of dollars and emerge a fashionista. It takes savvy and skill to look good on a budget of $37.99.

This is my ultimate fantasy: Stephen Spielberg will turn one of my books into a screenplay. The movie will be nominated for an Oscar, and I'll attend. No fuss about what to wear: I'll get out of the limo wearing the heavy maroon silk Balenciaga ballgown with a huge bow down the back, that fits perfectly and is hanging in my closet right now.

As I walk up the red carpet in the stunning gown, draped in a shawl of sari silk and carrying my antique beaded evening bag, the TV interviewer will gasp and ask about the dress. And I'll say, proudly, "It's vintage Balenciaga. I bought it at Goodwill. For eighteen dollars. Canadian."

That will be the equivalent of a year's worth of orgasms. It won't even matter if we win.

SUNDAYS

Sundays have been a battleground for me since childhood. My parents weren't religious; in fact, my father was furious at the biblical decree that everyone should rest on the seventh day, like God. He insisted on lots of outings and vigorous family activity — including the worst torture, family volleyball at the Y — while our neighbours put on gloves and hats and went piously to church.

My sense of being out of sync with Sunday was reinforced when I lived in Toronto as a young woman, in the early seventies. I grew up in the small cities of Halifax and Ottawa and was eager to begin adult life in this exciting metropolis, where the arts were blossoming in the most extraordinary way: theatres, galleries, clubs, new talent throbbing all over. Saturday nights were wild, dancing and drinking at The Riverboat, Grossman's, the Brunswick House, El Mocambo.

And then the next morning — what? It was Sunday in Toronto in 1973, and the city was dead. Everything was closed. Luckily, though, I didn't want to do much on Sundays. It took me all day to recover from Saturday night.

Later, I came to understand what Sundays, ideally, can mean, even to the non-religious. In France, one summer and fall, I worked at a L'Arche community, where people with and without disabilities live and work together. L'Arche is Catholic, although others are welcome, and this half-Jewish atheist tentatively joined in the community's religious activities, including going to church. To my surprise, I enjoyed it. The rituals of Catholic worship didn't mean anything to me, but the ritual of church attendance did. I realized how much that kind of structured contemplation, a spiritual stocktaking, is missing in modern life. The beauty of those L'Arche Sundays has stayed with me for many years.

Now I'm back in Toronto, this time with two teenagers. My daughter has no trouble with the concept of Sunday as a day of rest: she sleeps until mid-afternoon. Then she occupies the telephone and the shower, simultaneously if possible, for the rest of the day. My son spends the day outside practicing daring skateboard moves, not for his buddies, now, but for a coterie of admiring girls.

I myself am adjusting to the jazzy new, never closed Toronto, and to my newly old-fashioned self. The city recently opened for business on Sundays, and I don't like all that unlimited access. The bookstores being open was one thing, and the drugstores, but I draw the line at The Bay, and the thought of being able to buy liquor on Sunday — well, it just seems wrong, and I prefer not to do it. Not on religious grounds, you understand. I just don't see what's wrong with a day when most commerce shuts down.

Good Friday was that kind of day, like the old Sundays — calm, still, neighbourly. When I went for a walk, children were playing in the empty streets; people were strolling, sitting on their front porches, gardening, washing their cars, chatting. You could hear birds sing; you could hear yourself think. Why should speed and convenience overrule peace and quiet? Why should the great god Shopping rule the city, seven days a week?

Instead, here's my own simple Sunday ritual: I wake early and put on music by Johann Sebastian Bach; listening to the great man points me straight to heaven. I turn on my new little espresso machine. And then, to complete my joy, I open the front door. The *Sunday New York Times*, which has recently begun home delivery here, is waiting on my front step. I sit in my favourite kitchen chair gazing at the garden. My children are asleep; Bach is chorale-ing in my heart. I pour a coffee and open that great delicious slab of newspaper.

Even in this frantic modern world, it's possible to stop for a few moments of tranquility and thoughtfulness. There, in my kitchen on Sunday morning, a sense of the great glory of life abides awhile, with me.

BETH KAPLAN

Postscripts for Community:

Village spirit: *Just yesterday, I rode my bike to St. Jamestown Steak and Chops to buy a chicken for roasting. I eat less meat than I used to, but — please don't tell Paul McCartney, the world's most famous vegan — I still do. In the store, Mark came over for a hug and a chat, as usual. We've known each other for decades now. Two of his sons work behind the counter and will eventually take over the business, as he took over from his parents. Mark has made the place trendier, with prepared food and the servers in little caps with logos. My articles about the family — obituaries for both Terry and Doris, and this essay about the party — used to hang on the back wall; the one about Santo is there still.*

Dorothy, in her British way, called the main thoroughfare of Cabbagetown the high street. "I'm going shopping on the high street," she'd say. It's a privilege to feel so connected to this village where I live, in the heart of the metropolis. When we moved here, we could not have known that we'd acquired not just a dwelling and a garden, but a high street, and that over the years, some of the proprietors of its shops would come to feel like family.

Running: *The author, in her seventies, is no longer a gazelle. But she dances as often as possible, the best fitness method of all, as far as she's concerned.*

Goodwill junkie: *All the Goodwills in Toronto eventually closed down. I was in despair — would I have to buy NEW? — until another charity renovated a space around the corner and opened Doubletake Thrift Store.*

I go several times a month to chat with the kind Bengali women working there. Few treasures have been forthcoming. But I have enough, more than enough, and no longer have either time or need for that kind of stimulating consumption. One of the many, many benefits of getting old.

On the other hand, just the other day I did find a really useful jacket.

My activist daughter has declared war on capitalist consumption. She says she will no longer buy new clothes, ever. She wants only second-hand.

Proud mama here. The apple and the tree.

COMMUNITY

These essays appeared in:

Village Spirit, *Globe and Mail*, 1996
Radiohead, *Globe and Mail*, 1997
"Running," CBC, *This Morning*, 1998
"Baby Jesus Comes to Cabbagetown," *Tapestry*, CBC, 2003
"Sundays," *Metro Morning*, CBC, 1998

FRIENDS, LOVERS,
AND SIGNIFICANT OTHERS

Instructions for living a life:
Pay attention.
Be astonished.
Tell about it.

Mary Oliver, "Sometimes"

OLD FRIENDS, HERE AND GONE

F our old friends — Suzette, Jessica, Isobel, and I — got together the other night for the first time in many years. We met at university in 1967, slender teenaged virgins with long straight hair and miniskirts. And now here we are, somehow — when did this happen? — middle-aged. We jabbered and cackled, recalling our excesses, the crazy times, wild travels, love affairs, one-night stands. Suzette pointed out that we were the only generation of girls to have had such sexual freedom. The women before us didn't have the pill, and the ones after us had STDs and AIDS. We weren't sure, now, if our sexual freedom had been such a positive liberation. But at least it didn't kill us, as it killed so many of our gay friends.

And our thoughts turned, as they always do, to Bob.

Also at our university decades ago was a prickly young visionary named Robert Handforth. Bob was beautiful, tall, and lean, with overwhelming talent and drive and a startling prescience about everything in the arts. How did a man who grew up in the suburbs of Ottawa always know the cutting-edge latest in art and design, theatre, music, architecture, fashion? He was almost too far ahead of his time. One year he entered a university drama competition with a multimedia play he wrote, designed, and directed himself. He lost to a tired Pinter one-act.

Bob wore the first jean suit I'd ever seen, lived in the first loft, and collected camp fifties artifacts like lava lamps and ceramic black panthers long before anyone else. He attracted and championed a stimulating, eccentric group of friends, most of them artists like himself. We were all aware, even then, that to be an anointed friend of Bob was to be part of a select group. The four of us didn't know until our get-together, though, how much he'd actually changed our lives, how his shoves had moved us in the direction he thought we should take. A prize-winning production he directed led six of his protégés, including two of us, to enter the professional theatre.

BETH KAPLAN

With our next bottle of wine, we delved into our growing awareness of his homosexuality. Even in our late teens, hard as it is to believe now, not one of us knew anyone openly gay. Bob himself resisted coming to terms with his sexual identity. Early in our friendship he and I were wild about each other, and I could not understand, then, why our love didn't work out. We tried. A few years later, I learned why.

It was a long time before Bob accepted, if he ever did, both his own gifts and his anti-social limitations. He was unforgiving and judgmental with everyone, but especially himself. I always thought he'd accomplish much more if he'd just relax and let himself be. But he was a perfectionist who could not relax.

Bob turned into Robert, working in the theatre and the visual arts in Toronto, and then as an arts functionary at the Canadian consulate in New York. When in the mid-eighties I heard of his diagnosis, I was busy with small children; AIDS was a horrendous tragedy I tried to shut out. During his illness we four, though out of touch with each other, had at different times been to see him in his dusty Upper West Side apartment. In 1987, I flew in to New York for a quick visit with family and arranged to have lunch with Bob. He suggested we go to Barney Greengrass, a famous New York fixture, but when we arrived, there was a long lineup outside. Bob, furious, began to rant about the crowds in New York; he wanted things to be perfect for me. To calm him, I suggested that instead of waiting, we buy lox, sturgeon, and bagels and take them to his apartment, so we did.

But when we got there, I realized my mistake. His flat was small and dark, littered with pill bottles. And this was the early days of AIDS; no one knew if this murderous virus could be transmitted in ways other than sexually. I was suddenly terrified, thinking of my kids, fearing infection from Bob's plates, glasses, cutlery. My rational brain knew these thoughts were silly, but I could not quell my anxiety. We had a short, tense lunch, and I escaped into the sunshine as quickly as I could.

That was the last time I saw or talked to one of my great loves, a man whose encouragement of my acting talent had changed my life. He died a year later, aged thirty-nine.

How the memory of my ignorance and insensitivity saddens me. The others, too, deeply regret they didn't do more to help him.

As people of my generation do about John Lennon, we've never stopped wondering what Bob would be doing these days, what he'd be thinking. What he'd make of us. We all feel his critical eye, still. He boasted about each of us to the others, but he also was sure we could do better. To the end, Bob was uncompromisingly blunt about himself and everyone else.

We will never know what all the brilliant young men who vanished in that plague would have given the world. But, the four of us said, we can remember. We decided to meet at least once a year from now on, to celebrate our renewed friendship and our friend. As we said good night, I was perusing my companions with an eye for beauty, originality, style, taste, line. I knew where that eye had come from. They have it too.

The next morning we all received a startling email, sent out of the blue by our university schoolmate David. David was another of Bob's great comrades; we'd resolved to invite him to our next Robert Handforth memorial get-together.

"Today was my fifty-fifth birthday," David wrote. "I began it dreaming of Bob. He hadn't gained a pound. His face was unlined. His hair was radiantly sandy and he hadn't lost any of it. 'You haven't changed a bit,' I exclaimed to him. He grinned indulgently. I woke up laughing with delight."

Our irascible, self-deprecating friend would not have believed he'd be so missed. That nearly twenty years after his death, he would matter as much as ever.

But you are, Bob. You do.

SISTERHOOD

few weeks ago, on a sunny Sunday morning, I was part of an important annual event, a five-kilometre run and walk through the deserted streets of downtown Toronto. The event benefits research into breast cancer and has been growing steadily. When the starting gun finally boomed this year, 12,000 people began to move.

I've done the race before and usually think, while running, about my mother and my cousin Barb, long-term survivors of breast cancer. This year, though, a famous stranger was on my mind: Linda McCartney, wife of Beatle Paul, who died this spring of breast cancer, at the age of fifty-six.

Linda's death seemed wrong purely on medical grounds; she was vigorous and youthful, a vegetarian with a self-consciously healthy lifestyle. We've all seen pictures of Linda and Paul mucking about on their farm in Scotland, with children, horses, and sheep dogs, no visible stress, the freshest air and food possible. And her husband, one of the richest men in Britain, was there nothing he could do? Nothing. Neither healthy farm life and veggies, nor all the money on earth, could save her. What hope then for us stressed and ordinary mortals, living in smoggy cities, eating additive-laced burgers, without the benefit of limitless wealth and fame?

Besides forcing me to reflect gloomily on my own mortality, Linda's death also reminded me of the great bond we once shared. For some time, Linda and I felt the same way about the same man. In 1964 and '65, I dreamed constantly, hungrily, about Paul McCartney, and wrote reams of stories about us as a couple, which progress from him helping me with my arithmetic homework, to us roaring around Europe in his Aston Martin. Mostly, though, we're married and sitting by the fire, and he is singing to me.

Unfortunately, the closest I came to Paul McCartney was the eighth-row centre of a Beatles concert, where I screamed and waved his picture and he smiled down, right at me; whereas the closest Linda came was that she married him and had his children and lived with him for thirty years. Oh, well. Though she got him, we both loved him. There's a sisterhood in that.

I hated her back then, of course, though not as viciously as I'd hated Paul's first girlfriend, Jane Asher. Jane only wanted Paul's money and fame, that was sure, whereas my pure love was for his poetic musical soul. But then along came Linda. She was a groupie, we all knew that, a flaky American photographer who insisted, God help us, on singing with Paul's band, banging the tambourine. It was embarrassing; how could Paul permit it? Linda's singing was better than Yoko's, that was the only good thing you could say about it.

Linda's music making, and marriage to Paul, didn't concern me at all once real men appeared in my life. I went through an image change, too, recanting my love for the cute Beatle. It was now clear John Lennon was the interesting one; cool girls with insight and depth of character had chosen John. How could I have been so shallow? Paul's post-Beatles records were so ... cheerful. Yes, he often wrote every song on the album and sometimes played all the instruments himself: many kinds of guitars, keyboards, wind instruments, even drums. But the content, over and over, was lightweight, about love. He and Linda seemed to spend their lives in Wellington boots birthing lambs, when they weren't getting arrested somewhere in the world for marijuana possession. Meanwhile, John and Yoko were doing important things, like lying in bed agitating for peace.

But through the years, as the McCartneys and I aged together, I realized how wrong my impression was of them both. Linda was a strong, idealistic, kind-hearted woman who found her niche as a photographer, made an important contribution to the causes of animal rights and vegetarianism, and went on standing by her man with her tambourine, no matter what we thought.

And I now take enormous pride in being an almost lifelong Paul girl. My favourite Beatle, beneath his occasional sappiness, has a musical heart of breathtaking originality, lyricism, and force. Sir Paul McCartney, with and without John Lennon, has produced some of the most beautiful melodies ever written.

And while he did so, unlike almost all his rock star colleagues, he remained passionately in love with the same woman. He and Linda fashioned that rare thing, a long-lived, visibly happy and mutually fulfilling marriage. Despite their wealth and goldfish bowl life, they raised their children normally, with all going to local public schools. Their second child Stella, now famous in her own right as a fashion designer, speaks with down-to-earth respect and fondness of both her parents. It's hard to accept that when she says "my dad," or when I see a picture of a grief-stricken, jowly man with grey hair, it's actually the baby-faced boy who sang in my heart so long ago. Yesterday.

On Paul's latest CD, released last year, there are, as usual, several exquisitely tender love songs. His teenage son James plays a great guitar solo on one track. And there, singing in the background, is Linda.

"And if I only had one love/ Yours would be the one I'd choose," Paul sings.

"You and me together/Nothing feels so good," he sings.

She seemed to have everything a woman could want, but Linda McCartney died in April, of breast cancer, at the age of fifty-six. This year, I ran for her, and for those who lost her.

CHALLENGED

Once more, my thoughts have turned to Tracy Latimer. Soon the courts will retry Robert Latimer, her father, who four years ago killed his daughter Tracy "out of love and compassion," because he believed her severe disabilities caused her unspeakable pain. Most of us cannot imagine the toll that raising a child with such brutal disabilities takes on a parent, how heart-rending it must be.

The state, not without a great deal of soul-searching, found him guilty of second-degree murder and sentenced him to life in prison with possible parole in ten years. They will soon reconsider that decision.

We know Tracy's body was terribly deformed by cerebral palsy. She couldn't feed herself, walk, or speak, and had suffered a series of excruciating operations. We heard the agonized empathy with which her father says he viewed her struggles.

What we will never know or hear is how Tracy, twelve-year-old Tracy, felt about her life.

I know a little how my friend Don feels about life. Don is nearly as severely disabled with cerebral palsy as Tracy was, so damaged by complications during his birth that his parents were advised to put him immediately into an institution, because caring for him at home would be too gruelling. Don also cannot walk or feed himself. He needs to be lifted into bed, onto the toilet, back into his wheelchair; he has to be dressed, clothes stretched over his rigid, ungainly limbs. Don can talk, though his speech is so slurred it takes a long time to understand him. His parents were told he would live fifteen years, at most. His internal organs, crushed by the convolutions of his body, would simply give up.

This year, in his usual fashion — a banquet and a few stiff drinks — Don celebrated his forty-fifth birthday. He was with his four younger brothers, enjoying pineapple chicken balls at his favourite Chinese restaurant, when across the room, an attractive young woman stood up and waved at them. The brothers sat up in anticipation. The blonde crossed over to Don's wheelchair, threw her arms around him, and gave him a big kiss. "Don, I've missed you so much!" she said.

After she left, one brother asked, "Don, do you even know who she is?"

"No ... and ... don't ... tell ... Dad!" Don replied with a grin. The five brothers have always kept each other's secrets.

The success of Don's life is in every way a tribute to the limitless devotion of his parents. When he was born in 1952, children with disabilities were routinely consigned to large institutions for the rest of their lives. Parents who opted to keep their youngsters at home had no support services.

Despite the myriad difficulties involved in raising their eldest son at home, his father and mother only once considered putting him in an institution. They made the journey to the huge facility then serving the province's mentally and physically challenged.

"One look at that place," says his dad, "and we just turned around and brought him home."

He and his wife want no special credit for their years of caregiving. Don is their son, that's all there is to it.

"A family with a handicapped child," goes the glum saying, "is a handicapped family." There's no doubt Don's disabilities changed the course of his family's history. His father, retired from the gas station he ran for many years, unsentimentally points out a piece of land now worth a fortune and recalls that he was once offered it for a pittance. Even such a small amount, for a family with steep medical bills, was too much. Constant sacrifices were necessary to accommodate the family's most vulnerable and demanding member.

Don's younger brothers, all hard-working men with good jobs and families, have special qualities because of their childhood with a sibling as helpless as their oldest brother. They're conscientious fathers, confident and tender with infants; they know how to look after themselves and others. Humorous, reliable, they're seldom discontented or restless. As one said, "We were never like other kids, whining 'I wish I had that toy.' We lived with a brother who had so little. The unfairness of it."

That brother, despite his blurred speech and contorted body, has always had a powerfully assertive personality. Furious when his one-year younger brother left home for university, he insisted it was time he, the oldest, leave home too. Once again, the family did a search through local institutions. The best they could find was the extended care wing of the local hospital, which holds mostly the very old and patients with degenerative diseases. Against his parents' wishes, determined to be independent, Don moved into the hospital, where he stayed for nearly twenty years.

There he became involved with People First of Canada, founded in 1973 to encourage the mentally and physically challenged to live independently in their own communities. At first an avid fundraiser and "carwash captain," Don was eventually made president of his local chapter. Thanks to a new local innovation, the Handy Dart wheelchair van, he led an active community life himself, often out for coffee or, more likely, a drink with friends and family. At a People First conference at Whistler, Don fell in love with Debbie, who also has cerebral palsy. They exchanged rings, and although she lives in Vancouver, Debbie has come several times to visit him in Vernon. At parties they dance with each other, their chairs steered by caregivers.

Don has always lived with chronic pain, as Tracy did. Once there was talk of an operation to straighten his spine, to give his compressed organs some room. The twelve-hour operation would have left him in a body cast for six months. At first eager, Don ultimately decided against the ordeal. He wanted to stay right where he was, in his new home.

After years of lobbying, phoning, writing letters, introducing their son to provincial representatives, his parents finally persuaded the authorities to build a group home in the small B.C. town. Don's bungalow was designed to accommodate wheelchairs, with a central, low-slung kitchen and an extra-wide bathroom. He has lived there for six years now, with three companions and their caregivers, in as normal a family atmosphere as is possible under the extraordinary circumstances. He has his own room, the surfaces crammed with family pictures, the walls covered with posters of fellow British Columbian Pamela Anderson in a bikini. In the evening, when they're not barhopping in the Handy Dart, the housemates warm themselves by the fireplace. People drop in to visit. My friend sits in his new wheelchair, the cat squeezed in beside him, his rye disappearing slowly. His face is blissful.

Though Don's life may look limited and pain-wracked to us, not once has he complained about the fate that assigned him his twisted body. He simply kept asking for what he needed: lots of time with family and friends, a free local bus service for everyone in a wheelchair, and a group home with a fireplace and a cat.

And that is what he has.

YOUNGER MAN

admired his pale muslin curtains, and he said, "Thanks, I sewed them myself." Not the kind of man I was used to.

But then this man — my boyfriend, for now — is from another generation. Nineteen years younger than I am, he is different from men in their mid-fifties, my age. Clichéd as it is, I have seen him cry. He is unashamedly emotional, he talks about his feelings, is concerned about my feelings and listens when I talk. He even remembers what I have said. I know because he has quoted me later, word for word.

Viewed rationally, our affair makes little sense. People look, trying to figure out what we are to each other. When we first realized what was happening between us, it was harder for him than for me. For me, what a coup — a vigorous young buck. For him, what? A lover only ten years younger than his mother. He confessed early on that having feelings for an older woman worried him.

"Does it mean," he fretted, "there's something wrong with me?" Yes, a voice in me replied. You should be with a lovely young woman with a firm body and unlined skin; you should make a future together.

"Love comes in all shapes and sizes," is what I said out loud. "There's no explaining it."

But he should have a family, children of his own; he needs someone younger. And I need to find a more suitable partner. The problem is, I want one just like him.

Well … not completely like him. An older man would be more settled, with more options and freedom, more worldly sophistication, probably more money. An older man would know himself and have answered lots of questions. He would be more or less done, as I am or will be soon, with child-rearing and career anxiety, able to relax and put things in perspective. That would be good. But where will I find a man over fifty who loves to dance, who writes long emails full of chatty affection, who is trusting and funny, playful and tender and careful with carbs? Who, while we're at it, has a thick head of hair and a lean, strong body?

He was a volunteer fitness instructor at the Y. I took his class every other week for two years, gazing at him appreciatively, as at other male instructors; there's a lot of gazing at the Y. But there was no one quite like him. A friend of mine remarked, after his class, that she'd never before been thanked for doing push ups; he always says thank you to his students after push ups. It would never have occurred to me that something could grow between us, but when, by chance, we ran into each other several times outside the Y, I couldn't help but notice how interested he was in my work and life. How widely he seemed to smile before class, when I appeared in my running shorts. Was he friendlier to me than to other sweaty women? I hoped he was.

And then I realized no, he couldn't possibly have singled me out; I didn't even know how to smile at a man any more, let alone flirt. Divorced for over fifteen years, I'd had only one troubled relationship and a few brief, invisible flings in all that time. My single status had led me to hate the word used against single people like a bludgeon — "we." All those couples, stuck to each other, going everywhere chained into pairs — how conventional and boring. I loved seeing movies alone, free to digest in silence afterwards. Travelling alone was the best way to see new places, meet new people. Besides, I was busy working and raising children. No time for romance. No interest.

But this younger man warmed me. We took to bantering. One day, at the end of his fitness class, I dared myself to make a move, and walked from where I stood by the mats mopping my brow to where he stood in the centre of the room mopping his. We chatted, joked. I said, "We should have coffee some time." It was the first time in my life I'd made an opening gambit like that, aggressive to my generation, perfectly normal to his.

We had coffee and discovered we'd seen all the same obscure documentaries; we both love documentaries. I waited for him to tell me about the inevitable girlfriend, but he didn't. We exchanged email addresses. There was no harm, surely, in us becoming friends and seeing a movie or two together. We saw a documentary, had brunch and a drink and supper, went dancing; we walked a lot, and talked a lot. Despite mutual reservations, we grew closer.

Now we are lovers and companions, and in a month he is returning to his country on the other side of the world. He had made plans to leave before we began seeing each other, and he is still going. And I support his decision. I know exactly where I am and what I have to do; he has it all to figure out — work, past loves, future. Ill at ease with the language and customs of Canada, where he's lived for the past four years, he misses all that is familiar, and so, temporarily or for good, he is going home. He joked that if I came to visit, he would not introduce me to his Muslim parents.

"The age difference would not be the problem," he said. "The fact that you're half-Jewish would be the problem."

Perhaps he'll find a wife there and make a family. I can see the dark-eyed babies that he and some lucky woman will make; what a lively father he'll be. And I will send a wedding present; baby gifts.

Or maybe not. Maybe he will come back because there is no one quite like me, no one who understands and cares for him as I do, who is as open and supportive, because I have spent a lifetime getting here, to this place of relative peace. There are advantages to aging.

"I thought older people were different," he said once, "but they aren't. You're really about seventeen. You have a teenager's heart."

Somewhere inside, my teenaged heart knows that, even if he comes back from overseas, there's no future for us as a couple; the differences are just too great. But he has reminded me, after all those single years, of the pleasures of relationship, of going places with a companion, of someone caring where I am and what I'm doing. I'll miss that. I will miss him.

But it will be a pleasure and, yes, even a relief to reclaim my independence and solitude.

Is there something wrong with me?

DAD AT THE END

I'd flown to Edmonton yet again. As my father lay half-asleep one afternoon, he muttered that his feet were always cold, and I pulled back the bottom of the blanket. The skin on each slender foot was mottled and papery, the toes perfectly graded in length, just like my toes. I took his freezing feet in my hands and began to rub, to warm them. It was hot outside, for June.

As I kneaded and stroked, he sighed with pleasure.

"Thank God for those feminine genes," he said, with eyes closed. Which, for him, was pretty close to "I love you." Close enough for me.

Ten months before, my father had telephoned. I was standing at the back door of the old Toronto house he'd recently helped us buy, watching my shrieking children running through the sprinkler.

Dad never called. Family communication was my mother's domain.

"I have something to tell you, Bethie," he said. I knew instantly. Standing on the threshold, watching my kids crash naked and joyful through cold water, I strained to hear my father's voice long distance.

"They've found something," he said.

The scene outside blurred. No. Nothing bad could happen now. My life, so chaotic and unhinged during my twenties, had just settled into this unimaginable domesticity — husband and children, Victorian wreck of a house, backyard with sprinkler. They were all that mattered. Until now.

"There are good cancers and bad cancers," he was saying. "This is not a good cancer."

A scientist, he knew these things. My throat clenched, tears rolling. He could not leave me now. We still had so much to fix.

"I'll come to Edmonton," I said, keeping my voice steady. "When should I come?"

"The doctors are doing their job," he said. "Don't worry, Pupikina. You get on with raising my grandchildren."

In a photograph my husband had taken six years before, the day after the birth of our first child, I'm in a hospital bed, dazed and laughing, holding a tiny mysterious parcel wrapped in white. My dark-haired, dark-eyed dad is on his knees on the floor beside me, hands held up in supplication.

"Bella Madonna!" he's saying. "I worship at your feet."

Dad was a geneticist, and there, in my arms, was his immortality. Even by her second day, this dark-haired, dark-eyed daughter was combative, social, and impatient — just like him.

****

"You're a neanderthal," my father snapped, when, at thirteen, I confessed my passion for the Beatles. "A conformist!" He wanted me to worship Wolfgang Amadeus Mozart, like he did. During the Fab Four's first appearance on *The Ed Sullivan Show*, as I sat transfixed in front of our small rented television, he stood snarling behind me. "Yeah yeah yeah," he howled in derision. "Yeah yeah yeah!"

At his sixtieth birthday celebration nearly two decades later, he requested one of his favourite Beatle songs, "When I'm Sixty-Four." Whirling my mother around the kitchen, he crooned the lyrics about needing and feeding. Long before, to my astonished gratification, he'd admitted he was completely wrong about their music.

At the age of sixty-four, this man who adored everything about France — food, wine, people, language — went to Paris for an ecstatic visit. While there, he found himself unable to eat with his usual gusto, and then at all. On his return, only because my mother insisted, he went to see a doctor, to hear the diagnosis he'd dreaded all his life. Cancer. Cancer of the stomach.

What irony, I thought, and perhaps everyone who knew him thought. This was a man who lived for his stomach, who shovelled in food as if the next meal might never come, accompanied in recent times by vintage wines with names nearly as precious to him as those of his family: Corton-Charlemagne, Côtes de Beaune, Clos de Vougeot. He had at last, not long before, been able to fashion a wine cellar, a cool basement stash for his precious bottles, to be shared with those of similar discernment during a gourmet repast.

And now his appreciative stomach, his lifelong companion, had betrayed him.

****

At twenty-one, I was attending theatre school in London, England. On his way to a conference, Dad came to visit me. A friend lent us her car, and we set off north, to the Edinburgh Festival.

Our relationship had been so contentious and painful that for years, we hadn't spent even an hour alone together. Yet here we were, on the road for four days. I made him surrender his watch, so he was forced to slow down and relax, and he let me choose all the plays we'd see, including a musical by an unknown composer named Andrew Lloyd Webber.

I'd hoped this trip would be an opportunity for us to finally get to know each other, but there was a problem. Years before, my mother had claimed me as her confidante. She'd told me all about the passionate affair she was having, at that moment, with the young husband of a colleague of Dad's, a bearded musician much nearer my age than hers. Recently, she'd even asked me to vacate my London room for a weekend, so she and her lover could meet there for a tryst. I didn't know if Dad knew, and even if he did, it was obviously not something we could discuss.

As I struggled to keep her secret, there grew between my father and me, mile after mile, a thick barrier of silence about things that mattered. We talked about the weather in Scotland, the festival, the quality of our last meal and where to eat next, but not about our past together, and not about Mum. Once, while Dad filled up the car, I bought chocolate bars and stole into the bathroom to cram them into my mouth. Anything to keep myself quiet.

On the highway back to London, he spoke, his voice solemn. "Pupikina," he said, his favourite nickname for me, a mixture of Yiddish and Italian. "I know for some years I was hard on you. I hope you know I did love you all that time. Even if I didn't show it."

To acknowledge, at last, what a mean, critical bully he'd been! I wanted to pummel him. No, you sure as hell didn't show it, I started to say but didn't.

But then, to allow himself to be honest and vulnerable. *There's no one like him*, I thought. *He's brave and generous, has spent his life battling the reactionary forces of darkness, to change the world for the better. No one understands him like I do.*

I revered him. Always had, even at the worst times, when I hated him too.

"I know you did, Daddy," I said, touching his arm. "Love you."

"And I, you," he said, eyes on the road, and we were once more silent. As if something had been taken care of and didn't need to be broached again. And it never was.

****

In my favourite childhood photograph, I'm fourteen months old, moving my unsteady feet by hanging onto the back of my stroller. Dad, in pyjamas and plaid housecoat, smiles down at me as he holds himself up inside a steel walker. He is twenty-eight, recovering from a near-deadly bout of polio, struggling to push his emaciated legs forward.

My father and I are learning to walk together.

****

Eleven months after his diagnosis, in early July, I arrived again at my parent's house and was amazed to see Dad standing unsteadily on the deck. My mother whispered that when he heard the taxi pull up, he'd insisted on being helped to his feet, so his daughter would find him upright and strong.

We spent afternoons watching Wimbledon. The tennis fans assembled: my brother, my mother, and her older sister, Do, who'd been there in Oxford, England in 1944, when my British mother and American father met, and who'd flown in now, to help. Dad, drifting in and out from his place on the sofa, pretended to take interest. Though not in much pain, he was thin and weak, his skin grey. We didn't know how much time he had left; the palliative care nurse had said it could be days, perhaps weeks.

Dad was worried about me. Over and over, I'd left my very busy husband and a babysitter to take care of the children, because there was nowhere more important for me to be than with my father. "Shouldn't you be at home with your kids?" Dad asked several times.

"They're fine," I assured him, and myself. When the sitter called to say Sam had fallen and split open his chin, needing stitches, I spoke to my boy on the phone several times, fretted, felt sick with guilt. But I did not go home. Dad needed me. Or perhaps, more, I needed him.

The usual family tensions were heaving underneath — my brother and I, who'd never been close, were struggling to remain civil under pressure. My mother was as frantic about everything as always, only more so. We all disagreed about Dad's medication, what, when, how much. Unlike the neurotics fussing around him, my socialist, atheist, activist father had become almost serene, like an apprentice Buddha.

"I've been given so much," he said the morning of July 5, looking out the window at Mum's garden, bursting with roses and raspberries. "I'm deeply grateful to have lived this long." He was sixty-five.

On television that night was scheduled *The Man Who Planted Trees*, a National Film Board animated film about a man who makes a huge difference to his community and to the world. I insisted we watch. "It's about leaving a legacy, Dad, like you have," I said, "founding the Grammar School, working for nuclear disarmament and to end the Vietnam War, advocating for science and all the rest."

At eight, I herded the family into the living room to watch the film, but not long after it began, Dad slowly stood up. "I'm too tired, Bethie," he said, and with his son's help he shuffled, step by painstaking step, up the stairs. After the program, my brother and I went up to check on him. He was feverish. Propping up the pillows the way he liked, I sat beside him, holding his hand, weeping. "You have two children who love you very much," I managed to say. He tried to squeeze my hand.

"The ... feeling," he replied, so softly I had to lean in to hear, "... is ... reciprocal." His eyes closed.

I went downstairs, to sob aloud without disturbing him.

Later, a friend of Dad's told us he'd been stockpiling morphine. We're now sure that this day, the man who'd planted his own kind of trees had made a decision. He did not want to linger long enough to lose dignity, and he took charge to see that he did not.

At midnight, he was unconscious, his lungs rattling. My mother got into bed and held him in her arms, and I hauled my mattress to the floor nearby, to be close if needed. By 5.30 next morning, we could see that only the oxygen machine, pushing air into his lungs through the tubes in his nose, was keeping him alive.

"He wants to go," sobbed my mother. "How can we help him?"

"The oxygen should be turned off," Do said.

No one moved. I went over to the machine, found the white switch, and pushed. The hissing stopped. A terrifying lack of sound. My father drew one laborious breath. One more. Then silence.

At that moment — my rational mind cannot explain it — the light in the room changed. I felt my father's spirit leave his body and soar out the open window. An atheist and a sceptic, like him, I knew for certain his life force had just escaped into the pink-gold early morning. And then, as certainly, I felt part of that essence turn back and flood my being.

As surely as anything in my life, I felt my father bequeath himself to me.

The feeling — difficult, beloved, marvellous man — is reciprocal.

RECIPE BOX

"**B**ut what about the family recipes?" my mother cries. "What'll happen to them if I have no kitchen?"

The recipe box, covered with butter smears and dusted with flour, is where she keeps her grandmother's scone recipe. Years ago, when I came home from the hospital with my infant daughter, Mum was waiting for us with a batch of hot scones. Soon, perhaps, she will never bake again. A sad thought for us both.

But she's in her eighties, with osteoporosis and serious heart problems. Though she still lives alone, in a suburban condo with a view of the Ottawa River, twice in the last weeks, Mum has made a panicked call to 911. She rejects the notion of a live-in or even a part-time caregiver. The companion who rushes from the adjoining building to accompany her to Emergency is her capable sister Do, who's ninety. I live an hour's flight away in Toronto and come whenever possible. My brother has a half hour drive to her place and is as attentive and helpful as a busy man can be. But now, we wonder if it's time to contemplate a move.

And so I fly in and make an appointment, just for an exploratory visit, at a retirement home downtown where a friend's mother lived happily for years. Mum, my brother, and I walk in with trepidation. We all love the sunny apartment where she lives now, and we remember the "home" where her parents ended up thirty years ago, with its sour smell of disinfectant, its lobby a parking lot of residents nodding off in their wheelchairs.

But in this lobby, we see vigorous seniors chatting with each other, smiling staff greeting residents by name, an elderly man playing a grand piano. "It's good you came now," says the manager who gives us a tour, "while you have a choice." Most importantly, we learn a nurse is on duty twenty-four hours a day, and there are cords on the walls to summon help. Though we like the communal spaces, the first apartment he shows us is poky and drab. My heart sinks. But then he opens the door of the next. It's a small but bright and elegant one-bedroom, with white carpet and big windows overlooking the river.

Then and there, we pay a deposit to hold the place for two months, while Mum makes up her mind. We return the next day to learn about the activities and outings, the library and the Scrabble club, and to have lunch in the restaurant-like dining room. Mum eats heartily while eavesdropping on animated conversations and laughing with the friendly waitress. My mother has lost thirty pounds in the last years. It's great to watch her eat.

Back at her place later, however, what we're facing dawns on us both. After my father's death more than two decades ago, Mum eventually sold their four-bedroom house to move here. She endured the loss of many much-loved possessions to facilitate the change and still pays for a packed storage unit she never visits. Now we're considering a move to two small rooms with no kitchen. Around us are cupboards overflowing with kitchenware, toppling stacks of books, newspapers, and magazines, closets stuffed with clothes and shoes, the walls covered with art. To list just some of her collections: eggcups, letters, tools, shoe shining equipment, knitting and sewing equipment, art books and painting gear, sheet music, pots and boxes, calendars, brooches, old English pottery, and old English silver, especially spoons. Many, many spoons.

This woman lived through the privations of World War II in England; she throws nothing away. How to clear out of here and squeeze into that tiny space? Would it be worth the effort and stress?

"Just the move might kill me," she says gloomily.

"Yes, or it might give you a new lease on life," I reply cheerily, pointing out the possibility of new friendships, life downtown with outings to the art gallery and theatre, to the market and shops. I remind her of one of my father's favourite sayings: "To choose is to renounce." If you choose this, I say, yes, you'll renounce space, autonomy, and a lot of stuff. But you'll gain something vital: safety. "You'll be safe," I say.

She won't be safe; that's a lie. We all know what's coming down the pike, sooner for her than for most. But she'll be safer. I will sleep better, knowing she has help nearby. Am I pushing for this difficult move only for my own peace of mind? Partly. But why, too, shouldn't this vibrant woman live fully while she still can? Why not enjoy these years with no dishes to wash or food to shop for and cook, with new friends and concerts and especially a built-in nurse?

We face a mountain of hard decisions, downsizing, packing, and relocating if she says yes, and ongoing anxiety for all if she decides no. It's up to her. But before too long, I hope to visit my mother in her new, sunny, very small living room. I hope to meet the friends she has made and hear about her excursions and her Scrabble score.

And I'll bring fresh scones from the smeared, floury recipe box she has passed on to her granddaughter, my Anna, who loves to bake, and who one day will have to help me face hard decisions of my own.

Postscripts for Friends, Lovers, and Significant Others

Sisterhood: Friends who know about my great love for Paul kept writing me after his unfortunate second marriage ended. "He's single!" "Time to make a move! You go, girl!" As if I could just telephone one of the world's most famous men, introduce myself, and ask him out for coffee.

I assured them, marriage is not the issue here. I do not want to wash Paul McCartney's socks, though it's sure some nice person is paid to do that for him. It's one of my life's dreams to meet him and tell him how much he has meant to me and countless others. But he is now married to Nancy, a fine strong woman who obviously makes him happy, and that is a wonderful thing.

I do need to point out that Linda was and Nancy is Jewish, from New York. And I — ahem — am half-Jewish and sort of from New York. Born and with much family there, at least.

But no.

Challenged: When he was fifty-three, Don was devastated by the sudden heart attack death of his beloved father. The two were so close that it was hard to imagine one without the other. Don began to suffer acute anxiety attacks, and during one, his shrunken lungs simply could not bring in enough air. Those close to him felt his spirit had at last given way; he didn't want to go on without his dad.

Don's extraordinarily rich life was a tribute to the unceasing love and care of his parents, brothers, sisters-in-law, nephews and nieces, friends and caregivers. But most of all the success of Don's life was a tribute to the life force in the man himself. He may have been limited by his physical bonds, but there was nothing limited about his sense of humour and stubborn determination to live just like everyone else. There was nothing limited about his fierce and gallant heart.

These essays appeared in:

Old Friends, *Globe and Mail,* 2005
"Sisterhood," *Fresh Air*, CBC, 1998
Challenged, *Globe and Mail*, 1997
Younger man, *More Magazine*, 2010

LOOKING BACK

The past is never dead. It's not even past.

William Faulkner

Patience. Depth. Sit still and remember. Go there.

Wayson Choy

GROUPIE

Recently, my teenaged daughter Anna spent the weekend with her libido quivering, along with her vocal cords. The latest teen heartthrobs, the Backstreet Boys, were in town, and thousands of enraptured maidens, including Anna, went from airport to concert to TV studio, screaming out the anguished ecstasy of rock star love. Watching them took me back to 1964, when I flung myself heedlessly into the tidal wave of Beatlemania, not to surface for years.

To my relief, the Backstreet Boys are devoutly Christian young men, squeaky clean, or at least Brian is, the one Anna, happily, loves best. Perhaps members of this band are not luring sweet young things back to their hotel. When I was Anna's age, my adored Paul and the other Beatles seemed like nice safe boys but weren't, particularly. Groups like the Stones and the Doors made no pretense about what they were: musical raptors, hungry for adoring young females. And I myself was perfectly willing to be one of those young females — but only in theory.

In the summer of 1968, I was a seventeen-year-old waitress at the motor hotel my uncle was managing on the outskirts of Cornwall, Ontario, a town where, clearly, nothing ever happened. And then one night the fab British rock group, the Kinks, came through. Incredibly, without warning, they descended on my uncle's motel to spend the night. This event was pivotal in my life, a prime example of how things were to be for me, groupie-wise. The weekend the Kinks were in Cornwall, you see, I wasn't. I'd gone home to Ottawa for the first and only time that summer, to visit my parents.

On my return, all the other waitresses were hysterical with stories about what the Kinks had said, at whom they'd winked, their accents, clothes, and boots; there were hints of further activity through the night. I was so envious. While this far out thing happened, I was shopping for miniskirts with my mother. ("I think that's a sweater, dear, not a dress.") Bemoaning my lost opportunity, I never asked myself: the opportunity for what?

Later there were other opportunities, all equally vague and equally lost. One night at the El Mocambo in Toronto, I smiled so fondly at the washboard player of the Star Spangled Washboard Band that he came over and asked me out after the set. "Sure," I said. *Wow, he invited me out! The washboard player!* I sat waiting after the set, but it took him so long to appear from the dressing room that I got fed up and went home. Apparently, when he finally emerged, he was incredulous that I hadn't waited. Real groupies waited.

A few years later, living on the West Coast at twenty-four, I boarded a small plane from Vancouver to Victoria, followed by five exotic long-haired men. Sitting right next to me, it turned out, was the folk-rock star Tim Buckley, flying in with his band for a show that night.

We got right into conversation, Tim Buckley and I: folkies versus rockers, touring, his musical life, my acting life. He told me he lived in Venice and seemed amused, for some reason, when I asked if he spoke Italian. He was enthralling — intense, perceptive, almost shy, with deep dark eyes and a tangle of curls. As we landed, he said he'd leave me a ticket for the show, to come and see him after. How I enjoyed going up to the ticket wicket that night and saying, "Tim Buckley left a ticket for me?"

On stage he was disturbing, a jerky performer with a harsh, torn voice. He wore a buckskin jacket with very long fringe that whipped around his taut body as he crooned and belted and wailed.

Afterward, making my nervous way backstage — "Tim Buckley invited me, really!" — I was disconcerted to find a group of young girls already waiting. Were they real friends of Tim's, like me? We were led to a lounge where perspiring musicians were splayed out, drinking beer. The other girls giggled and flirted, one even climbing up on a guitarist's knee. I just wanted to talk to my pal. But he was slumped, unresponsive, certainly not eager right now for conversation. So I sat, trying to look attractive and interested, perky and keen.

We rose; there was going to be a party at the band's hotel. A silent distribution was taking place. The nymphet with the longest, blondest hair seemed to be with Tim. The manager, who had long black hair and a long curling mustache, seemed to have claimed me. At the hotel, he told me to come with him while he got something from his room. So, obediently, I went.

We stood in front of his door as he looked for his key. The thing was, he was wearing a jumpsuit covered with zippers, zippers on the sleeve, on the legs, on the behind, as well as the regular places. His key was inside one of those zippers, but he couldn't remember which.

As he unzipped more and more furiously, it dawned on me that perhaps something uncalled for was going to happen in his room. It certainly didn't look as if I was going to meet the nice Tim Buckley from before. I turned to this guy, who was bent over unzipping his ankles, and said, "I'd better go home now. Thanks anyway," and walked off. He shouted after me, cursing, still unzipping. At home, I got through to Tim in his hotel room and thanked him for the ticket. His speech was slurred. I don't think he knew who I was.

Tim Buckley died the following year of a heroin and morphine overdose near his home in Venice, California. He was twenty-eight.

Was it his melancholy dark eyes and quick mind that so attracted me, or the sexual allure of his music and his fame? I don't know and am grateful I didn't have to figure it out at the time. Just as I'm glad my Backstreet Boys fan could adore her group through the plate glass windows of a television station.

It was a close call, though, with the Kinks. At seventeen I was a virgin, naive, needy, polite. There might not have been enough zippers. And then this would be quite a different kind of tale.

ON THE ROAD AGAIN

Before the start of my years as an actor, I had a fantasy about theatre life — that it would involve a beautiful old theatre and a dressing room with my name on the door. But my first acting job was a tour. My second acting job was a tour. And my third. Actors now, I learned, just like in olden days, find themselves mostly not in beautiful old theatres, but on the road.

At nineteen, while in third-year university, I was thrilled to be cast without auditioning in a professional four-month touring show, and the following year in another. *This is so easy!* I thought. *They offer you work, give you an Equity card, and pay you really well.* I auditioned for a prestigious British theatre school and was one of two Canadians accepted that year. Obviously, this was my calling. Fame and fortune would surely follow.

But back in Toronto, reality hit, in the form of endless demeaning rounds of auditions with every other actress my age and type. Hours at a commercial audition for Heinz baked beans, waiting to stand in front of the casting director and cry, "You tell 'im, Frank!" with goofy enthusiasm. (The job went to an actress goofier and more enthusiastic than I. But when the beans ad eventually aired, the line was spoken by a man.)

The work I did find most often involved touring. During my eleven years as a professional actor, I did nine tours. Small tours, big tours, looong tours. Even my theatre school class in London ended up travelling about; we performed a medieval morality play on a cart pulled by Clydesdale horses. The play portrayed the Massacre of the Innocents, and during one show, as I battled the soldier who wanted to tear the infant from my arms, I realized the bundle representing my baby had fallen to the floor, and I was standing on it. Here's the first law of touring: even if you're standing on your baby, keep going.

I graduated to school tours. We performed for Grades 7, 8, and 9, which meant sometimes we couldn't hear ourselves on stage for the sound of hormones rushing through the audience. One of the plays was an adaptation of *Under Milk Wood* by Dylan Thomas, done as a foot-stompin' Canadian folk drama with music by Gordon Lightfoot's evil twin. Luckily, one of my colleagues was comedienne Nancy White who has a finely tuned sense of the absurd, essential when you find yourself square-dancing to the poetry of Dylan Thomas before the incredulous eyes of Grades 7, 8, and 9.

That was bliss, however, compared to my next school tour, Greek tragedy on the West Coast. The script called for us to do a lot of chanting in ancient Greek: "*Zena the-on ton ariston a eysomy ay demi ...* " A Greek scholar came to rehearsals to correct us as we chanted, so our pronunciation would meet the standards of any ancient Greeks living on Vancouver Island. The women were costumed in demure tunics, and the men, bare-chested, wore little brown skirts. If you ever start to fantasize about the glamour of acting as a profession, imagine being a male actor in a miniskirt, performing *Oedipus* in ancient Greek in a high-school cafetorium in Nanaimo.

The tours kept coming my way, in that era of youth grants; back then, incredibly, the government doled out money to keep its young artists employed. One of my favourites was Mid-Air Summer Theatre in Brockville, which produced *Peter Pan* with a remarkably small and ever-shrinking cast. I, for example, played Mrs. Darling the mother, Curly, a lost boy, and Smee, a pirate, as well as tootling the Tinkerbelle sound effects on my flute and taking care of two injured cast members: our original Peter Pan, who was in hospital with acute appendicitis, and our original Wendy, who also landed in hospital because the awkward actor who replaced the original Peter Pan threw open his arms to show her how to fly, and broke her nose.

Next was raucous ACME Theatre, whose members wrote and toured a wild musical play about the history of our city, opening with a song that went, "Vancouver, Vancouver, it's a word that you can rhyme with 'paint remover.'" Another troupe, Theatre One, toured the interior of B.C. in a big red bus, in which the six of us got to know each other much too well, one a nudist macrobiotic health nut, another who ate anything in the vicinity of his mouth, a third who survived on a strict diet of cigarettes, illegal substances, and creamed corn.

During my brief hippie period, I joined the draft-dodgers, misfits, and geniuses of a counterculture theatre troupe from the Kootenays; they'd just received a grant to tour the province's prisons and mental institutions in their picturesque van which had no second gear. We rehearsed — and lived — on the top floor of the village Kiwanis Club, which had no running water, or heat, or furniture.

After my brief hippie period, I was glad to be offered a job by the big respectable Playhouse company, which operated out of a big respectable theatre. I ended up, of course, on tour, in a zippy, zany sex comedy about the antics of repressed university professors, which we took to the remote logging villages of northern B.C.

And then, the last, the mother of all tours: a new Canadian musical, sort of like "The Shumka Ukrainian Dancers meet *Othello*," which took four months to wend its way through every major cultural centre from Edmonton to Petrolia. I came to call our big cast of seasoned party animals Alcoholics Not So Anonymous. In Montreal, the handsome prankster who was our leading man had a run-in with some humourless Québécois police and did the show for some time with half his face mashed in. In Toronto, we all caught a terrible flu and had a mattress placed backstage so those of us aching and shaking with fever could lie down and die, until it was our cue to go on and sing and dance.

Was this really the work that would fulfill me? For the rest of my life?

Not long after, as my thirtieth birthday approached, I had a dramatic change of heart: I wanted to be a mother and a writer and stay put. I left the theatre and now labour over a hot stove and a warm computer. Both my jobs keep me in one place. Home.

These days, I'm deeply grateful that when ill, I'm not required to drag my body from bed and perform. Going to the theatre is like visiting a fascinating country where I once worked, where the citizens speak a language I used to speak fluently but no longer do. My good friend from London theatre school, Harriet Walter — we were considered similar types, tall brunettes, not standard beauties but striking, clever, strong — has had such a stellar career, she was made a Dame. We've continued to check in on each other's lives, me with children, teaching, and writing, she jetting around the world for TV and film and also writing several fine books. I turn on the television and there's Dame Harriet, side by side with the most famous actors in the business. Watching the well-deserved success of my friend gives me pride and pleasure, and not a drop of envy.

This immensely gifted, industrious artist enjoys the satisfaction of fame and, I hope, fortune. For me, a house that roots me in place. Family. Garden. These words on the screen.

A few years after quitting, I received a phone call from a director who wanted me to come to his theatre and act in a play. The play was by Molière, the theatre was in Thunder Bay, and the timing was Christmas. What a relief to thank him for the offer and turn him down. In my twenties, I would have gone. I would have left home and family to do Molière in Thunder Bay, at Christmas. An actor, in this country, has no choice but to roam constantly for work — to

LOOKING BACK

Regina, to Halifax, then Victoria, then Winnipeg. Hundreds of artistic nomads crisscross the land, giving all for the magic — dreaming of a dressing room with their name on the door, in the town where they actually live.

I, who gave up, whose journey now, with words, is solitary and inward, miss them, and honour them, and thank them.

L'ARCHE

*A*uthor's note: Please see the Postscript at the end of this section for a current re-assessment of Jean Vanier.

Not long ago, an invitation to a weekend-long party in the south of France landed in my mailbox. It read, "Soon the community of the Moulin de l'Auro will celebrate its twentieth birthday!" Just holding the letter, with its French postmark, took me back to the summer my life changed for good. When I worked at the Moulin de l'Auro, the community was brand new. After my stay there, I was brand new, as well.

In June of 1979, I was a twenty-eight-year-old Vancouver actress, quasi-alcoholic, single, and confused. Much wasn't right in my life, but I had no idea what was wrong or how to fix it. When the end of an acting job left some unexpected free time, I decided that since I'd never embarked on a post-college tour overseas, I'd do so now: take a quick jaunt through Europe and find myself. After brief but momentous stays in Holland, Greece, and Italy, however, I remained unfound.

My last stop was the south of France, for a short visit with my friend, Lynn. Years before, Lynn had gone to hear the Canadian visionary Jean Vanier speak about his life's mission, the founding of communities where people with mental and physical disabilities, and people without, would live and work side by side in a home-like environment. After listening to this eloquent man, Lynn had immediately volunteered to spend a year working at L'Arche (which means "the Ark"), the first of Vanier's communities in a village north of Paris. There she'd fallen in love with another volunteer, a Frenchman named Denis.

By the time of my visit with her, eight years after their wedding, L'Arche communities had sprung up around the world, and Lynn was the mother of three French children. Denis had recently founded a new community,

Le Moulin de l'Auro, an ancient mill and rambling stone house in the spectacular Provençal village of Gordes. I dropped in to spend a few days with my friends and their children, and left the village nearly five months later, transformed.

During my visit, one of the assistants working at the Moulin as a driver had to leave. Denis told me the men and assistants would be unable to go away on vacation if the position wasn't filled, and offered the job to me. *Are you out of your mind? I'm not a do-gooder,* I thought. I had absolutely no interest in or patience for people with disabilities. *Go home,* I said to myself, *grow up, get a job!*

Instead, I astonished myself by rescheduling my affairs long-distance and moving into the community.

My new circumstances were a horrifying shock, at first. I'd never known anyone with a great and obvious deformity, and my new housemates had deformities that were great and obvious indeed: Patrick, whose boxer's face was covered with cuts and swellings, the result of falls during his frequent epileptic seizures; Jean-Luc, with a small powerful body and a child's mind, subject to uncontrollable rages; Yannick, a huge slow man who rarely spoke; jerky Hughes, scowling François, handsome, psychotic Michel.

Within days, however, the first truth of L'Arche became apparent: some disabilities are immediately visible, and some only become visible in time. We assistants were just as handicapped — Vanier would say, "as wounded" — as Patrick and the others. We didn't have epilepsy or Down syndrome, but we were closed and unloving, or selfish, or greedy, or lazy, or frightened, or small.

I then learned the second lesson of L'Arche: the soul cannot help but grow in community. We ate together, worked, played, and rested together. This odd group became my family, with all that a family entails: one moment a desperate desire never to see these people again; the next, a need to help or be helped, to hear or be heard, to be with the others, in community.

After July at the Moulin, working every day with the men assembling door handles, learning to cook for twenty, learning that washing up for twenty can be a quick and pleasant chore with a cheerful group, I drove a number of us in the minibus to our August vacation, just like any other French family. The parents of one of the assistants had lent us an empty farmhouse in a sheep pasture. And there we lived for a month: four assistants and six disabled men, in the middle of a sea of sheep.

There are many indelible memories, but one stands out. During our last week there, we pitched a tent in a nearby field to give the men a chance to sleep outside, and one evening I went to camp with volatile little Jean-Luc and Yannick the silent giant. During the night a violent storm broke; lightning cracked the sky, and rain battered our shelter. Yannick snored serenely, but Jean-Luc was terrified. To calm him — to calm myself too — I held him in my arms until he fell asleep. The next day, beaming in the pale morning sun, he announced to the others in his halting speech that we were now married.

He followed me constantly, cooing, calling *"ma copine"* — my special friend. I tried to explain, the others tried, but he was firm: we'd hugged at night, and he knew from movies, that's what married people did. Though I turned away from him again and again, he kept reappearing by my side, hopeful, bewildered. We would move to the city, he told me, and he would drive a truck.

L'Arche had given us no guidance on how to deal with sexuality in the community, as if the issue did not exist. But I swore that never again, here or anywhere, would I be careless with loving gestures, or with love itself.

Back in Gordes we resumed the daily routine of the Moulin: door handles, cleaning, cooking, sitting together at a long table to eat and argue, talk and sing. Inviting the village to a party, we produced a play which starred silent Yannick as a tall talkative princess, with Jean-Luc banging out his own kind of music on a stringless guitar. As the season grew colder, my heart grew bigger. When I left, in November, I was overwhelmed with love for these men, who had taught me so much and were so beautiful.

A few years later, Jean-Luc became dangerous to himself and others, and had to be sent back to the hospital for a change in medication. Denis then had an inspiration. When Jean-Luc returned to the community, everyone called him by another name: Tom. His rages stopped. Jean-Luc may have been angry, but Tom wasn't. He was Tom for a while, and then he became Jean-Luc again, sunny as a child. When I came to visit after many years, he knew me right away. *"Ma copine!"* he called, with a smile that engulfed his face.

Happy Birthday, Moulin de l'Auro. May you have a joyous weekend celebrating the power and the glory, in sickness and in health, of community. Now that I'm so firmly found, I can't leave family and work to travel, so cannot be there, with you.

But on that weekend, as for the past nineteen years, you will all be here, with me.

POP

On this Mother's Day, I've been thinking about my grandfather, and about a trip I once took that made him a happy man.

In the mid-sixties, my father's father, a jovial self-made New York businessman we all called Pop, retired to Florida with my crabby grandmother. After she developed Alzheimer's, he cared for her faithfully until she died.

Born on the Lower East Side to penniless Jewish immigrants from a *shtetl* near Minsk, Pop was the favourite of his six brothers and sisters and the extended family because he was the kind of man who never failed to help a relative in need. All Pop himself wanted in his old age was a great-grandchild or three. His siblings were always boasting about their many great-grandchildren, and he had nothing to say. Of his two sons, the younger, my uncle Edgar Kaplan the world bridge champion, had married late and was raising Abyssinian cats. The other, my father, had produced a son and daughter, but neither of these disappointing specimens had settled down to make an old man proud.

Pop couldn't understand it, especially of me, the girl. I was getting old — twenty, twenty-three, twenty-eight! By twenty-eight, as far as he was concerned, I'd missed my chance to have a family.

But I didn't care. I had absolutely no interest in children. They were inconvenient, expensive, noisy, smelly, demanding. My life was good. I was free. Who needs a mate and babies, a mortgage, and a lawnmower? Sorry, Pop.

But a summer trip to see a friend in France spurred a change of heart. Lynn and I had been carefree students and then roommates and actors together at Carleton University in Ottawa. After graduation she'd gone to France and stayed, whereas I'd attended a prestigious theatre school in London and begun work as an actor in Canada.

Now I had a flourishing career and busy sex life and bachelor apartment, and she had three children in a little rented house in Provence, full of toys, laundry, and breadcrumbs. As a guest in her home, I struggled to relax; every time my friend and I sat down and tried to talk, one of her kids started to howl. She asked me to babysit for an afternoon while she got a haircut, and I hated every tedious minute. How did she do this boring job all day? A nightmare.

Late one evening, I impatiently followed my friend into the bedroom where her three were asleep. As she went from bed to bed, tucking them in, I stood in the doorway watching. The little beasts weren't their obstreperous, demanding daytime selves. Nestled in their cots and cribs, they were perfect, with perfect downy skin and perfect little bodies, each so luscious and so different.

There's pleasure in this motherhood thing, I thought for the first time. *There's tenderness and touch.* And a force so powerful struck me in the solar plexus that I nearly fell backwards against the door. My whole being flooded with need.

I want a baby, I thought. *My own baby.*

This cataclysmic realization was so bewildering, I thought my friend must notice something different in my face. But she didn't, and I said nothing.

The next day I noted how much Lynn's son resembled his father, not only in looks, but in personality. Denis was writing, the young son drawing, the two identical in stance, leaning over their papers, equally intent.

When you have a child, I thought, *something of you is transferred to a new human being. A new human being.*

In November, I returned home a new human being myself.

A long time later, it dawned on me that, as I stood watching Lynn with her children, Mother Nature had grabbed me by the collar and said, "You're twenty-nine, sweetheart. Enough fooling around. Time to do your job."

And I'd obeyed.

In March of the following year, I took my new boyfriend, who'd just become my fiancé, on a trip to Florida to visit my grandfather. Pop agreed, here was the ideal mate, but he was too discreet to hint about children or even a wedding. The old man at eighty-five was frail, easily tired, though still golfing every day in his pink and yellow polyester golfing pants. He was pleased with me, and proud. His granddaughter was at last doing what a woman should do, in his eyes.

"I thought you'd fall for someone like your daddy," he said, beaming, "but instead you've fallen for someone a lot like me!"

I didn't argue, though inwardly smiling at the notion that a hard-nosed, laser-focussed, driven American businessman in the rag trade, and a small-town Canadian, a producer in a tiny not-for-profit theatre, had anything in common.

A long time later, it dawned on me that he was right.

One momentous Saturday afternoon five months after our trip to Florida, the doctor confirmed I was pregnant. Though we'd not intended to become parents so quickly, my beloved and I were both elated. I had a good cry long distance with my mother. And then the overwhelmed prospective parents went out for dinner, to make plans and argue about names. At home, before bed, we each wrote a letter to Pop, giving him the news.

Mum called me the following day, Sunday. She wanted to tell me that the night before, unusually, Pop had telephoned her just to chat. So he learned right away about my pregnancy. He was overjoyed to hear about the baby, she told me, and insisted we get married immediately.

She said the centre where he lived had just called to inform her that his heart had stopped early that morning.

Pop didn't meet his great-grandchildren, my daughter and son, but he knew they were promised. In the years since, I've learned children do cost a lot and drive you crazy. And then they turn into teenagers.

And that with them, along with all the *tsuris* — a fine Yiddish word meaning trouble — comes a joy of unimaginable depth. They bring the most important gift of all: the hope that we, like this improbable planet, like the ants and the stars and the lilac about to bloom, will go on.

There are two new human beings here, Pop. For you. For all of us. For life.

1961

"**L**ook at this, dear," said my mother, sliding the *Halifax Mail Star* across the table. "Why don't you enter?"

She was so annoying, my mother, always full of energy and ideas. *Her* ideas, what she liked and wanted to do, not my ideas. Tennis lessons, sewing lessons, things I hated. I ate my poached egg in silence. Leave me alone.

"Go on, read it," she said. There'd be no peace until I did. It'd be time to leave soon anyway, to get the bus back to school.

She was pointing to a column called Ask Andy. Each week, Andy answered the letters kids had sent in, mostly boring questions about science. I hardly ever bothered to read Andy's cheerful answers. My father was a scientist, and his answers to my questions had shown me that everything to do with science was incomprehensible. But this week, Andy was announcing a contest for children nine to fourteen. I was eleven.

"Write about your favourite book in 50 words or less," it said, "and you could win a set of *Encyclopedia Britannica Junior!*"

Big deal.

But wait. I didn't even have to think about the answer. Opening a scribbler, I ripped out a page, and while still eating my egg, began to write.

"My favourite book is *A Little Princess* by Frances Hodgson Burnett," I wrote, and then stopped. How to describe this book and what it meant to me in only fifty words?

I'd just turned eight when we came back from a long stay in England, and I started Grade 4 at my new school, Tower Road. One day when my work was finished early, Miss Haines gave me permission to go to the books table in the corner of the classroom and pick a book. There was a brightly coloured series about some twins by the name of Bobbsey, which did not look interesting. About to reach for some animal stories, I saw a thick book with a dark-haired girl on the cover. *A Little Princess*. Back at my desk, I began to read.

Ten minutes later, the bell clanged for recess; the kids scraped their chairs and got ready to race outside. My body did not want to move. "Please, Miss Haines, I don't feel well. May I stay in this once?" I pleaded, and she nodded yes.

Bliss — time alone with the book and its heroine, Sarah Crewe, who was already my heroine. Sarah Crewe was wise beyond her years. She was not pretty, but that didn't matter to her. Sarah was clever, thoughtful, and honest. She read, and even when she was sad or frightened, she told stories.

The children came storming back. After recess was art class. The teacher, fat Mrs. Plunket with frizzy perm curls like my mother's Brillo pad, stood at the front of the room, showing how to draw perfect circles. Suddenly, I heard a loud distant noise and looked up. Everyone in the classroom was staring at me. Mrs. Plunket was pointing at me and roaring, "Look at her! Bold as brass, head in a book! In my class!"

Dazed, as if swimming to the surface from underwater, I shut *A Little Princess* and did my best to draw a perfect circle. If the teacher had tried to take the book away from me, I would not have let it go. The next summer, for my ninth birthday, I asked for my own *A Little Princess*. After keeping the first one for as long as possible, I'd had to put it back on Miss Haines's book table.

By then, I'd read the book so often, Sarah was like a best friend or even a sister. She and I felt the same way about loneliness and missing a father. Like Captain Crewe, my dad was handsome and funny, although mine did not cherish me the way hers cherished her. Sarah was way nicer — quieter, kinder, more generous — than I, but we both knew about being the odd one out and telling stories to make the shadows less frightening. There were many things in my life that scared me. Especially why my parents, who'd separated for a while in England and now were back together, sometimes got along and sometimes shouted with anger. They'd gone out to a party, my tall mother beautiful in her sparkly skirt and the red lipstick and Chanel No. 5 perfume she wore only at night, my father wearing a tie. In the morning, when I got up, my mother was sweeping up glass in the kitchen.

"Your father got drunk and was so horrible to me last night, Beth," she said, "that I drove home by myself and locked the door, and when he got here, he smashed the window to get in. Smashed this window," she said, as if I hadn't seen it, "and climbed in."

Couldn't my parents just get along calmly, like other people's parents? Sarah's mother was dead, and her father was very far away. My mother wasn't dead, just unhappy. And though my dad was right there, often he felt very far away too.

There was one scene especially; imagining it felt like a door opening in my chest. After her father's sudden death in India, Sarah, who'd been the wealthiest pupil at a London boarding school, is left with nothing. She's made to live in the bare, unheated attic, next to her friend Becky, the scullery maid. Sarah is always cold and hungry, but one day she's even colder and hungrier, because Miss Minchin the cruel headmistress is punishing her. She goes to bed trying to imagine food and warmth; imagining, as she always has, that she's a princess who must suffer bravely in silence, because others are worse off. But despair nearly overwhelms her.

During the night, a wondrous thing happens. The old man next door, who has noticed the thin waif with the intelligent face, sends his nimble Indian servant, his *lascar*, over the roof and into Sarah's room. While she sleeps, the *lascar* silently lights a fire and brings over soft blankets and food. She thinks she's still dreaming as she wakes, because she feels warm, and the room smells good.

But when her eyes open, she sees it's real. It's real, the warmth, the fire, the hot food waiting. She doesn't know where the miraculous gifts came from, but she accepts the fact that someone, somewhere, has noticed and wants to help. Someone cares about her. She brings in Becky and shares everything.

When Sarah walks into the classroom, Miss Minchin expects to see the child starving and frozen, truly humbled at last. Instead, Sarah's eyes are glowing, and her body is straight and strong. Miss Minchin is aghast; how can the child look like that when she has eaten nothing for so long? She whispers in fear to her sister, "Maybe she IS a princess, after all."

Sarah was indeed a kind of princess. And maybe — why not? I was one too.

I took another bite of egg and covered the white sheet with writing, with a bit of hesitation about my spelling.

"This book is about Sarah Crewe whose loving father dies pennyless, so she has to become a starved, overworked maid in the boarding school where she used to be the star pupil. Sarah survives with courage and imagination. By telling stories of bravery and strength and remaining true to herself in the face of the cruel headmistress, she triumphs over lonliness, hunger and despair. Sarah Crewe is my hero."

The piece was supposed to use at most fifty words; mine had sixty-nine so I wrote a note at the bottom: "I'm sorry this is a bit long but I love this book so much, I couldn't do it justice with less."

They'll like that, I thought, and ran to get the bus, leaving the essay on the table. It was splashed with egg yolk, but who cared, this was Mum's project, not mine. She must have mailed it in, because a month later, an official-looking letter came addressed to me. The set of *Encyclopedia Britannica Junior* was on its way.

My first thought was that they had made a mistake, and my second was, *It's that easy?*

A reporter from the *Halifax Mail Star* came to take my picture and interview me. By then the books had arrived, fifteen thick red and gold encyclopedias with all the information in the world stored in them. My father cleared the bottom row of his bookshelf, and we lined them up there.

"So, young lady, why did you pick *A Little Princess*?" the reporter asked, and I told him like in my essay, all again.

"Let's get a shot with one of the encyclopedias," the reporter said, and I stood holding one of the heavy books, trying to smile.

"You're only eleven, Beth." He wore a hat and was scratching with a pencil in his little notebook, like reporters in the movies. "Do you have any idea what you want to be when you grow up?"

"Well yes, I do," I replied. Of this, at least, there was no doubt whatsoever. I was writing all the time, had appeared in two stage plays, and was part of a drama group that improvised fairy stories every Sunday on local television. "I'd like to be a writer and an actress," I said.

"Ahhh, of course you would," he chuckled, smiling indulgently, shaking his head and putting down his pencil. "I was your age once, too."

****

"You're going to meet a famous man, kids," said Dad, as my family climbed into the Morris Minor. It was a sunny day in August 1961, and he was taking us to the north shore of Nova Scotia, to a town with the strange name Pugwash. A few hours later we stopped at an impressive mansion near the water with lots of green grass and lots of people, all of us there to meet Yuri Gagarin, the Russian spaceman, or as Dad said, cosmonaut. A few months before, Yuri Gagarin had been shot into space in a rocket and had circled the earth for a long time. The very first man in space. What had it been like to float around way up there, all alone, peering down at the earth very far below? What a brave man.

There were long tables with free food and drink, including Fanta that was my favourite and we were allowed to have as much as we wanted. There were speeches, and then we lined up to shake hands with Mr. Gagarin. He was a small man with bright blue eyes, sandy hair, wide cheekbones, a big grin, and an impressive green uniform with lots of badges and clinking medals. Daddy stood talking with him while the rest of us waited nearby, and then it was my turn. After we'd shaken hands, Mr. Gagarin laughed and ruffled my hair, and then he took off his hat and put it on my head. It fitted nearly perfectly. I was wearing the hat of the first man in space! And then he took it back and went on shaking hands, and I walked to the table to have an egg sandwich and more Fanta.

Daddy was with a group of men talking about world peace and Ban the Bomb. He was telling them about a letter he'd sent to one of his heroes in the peace movement, a famous professor called Bertrand Russell. Bertrand Russell wrote him a nice letter back, one peacenik to another. Dad had had the letter framed.

I didn't feel proud of my mother in the same way as Dad, even though she was part of a peace group too, the Voice of Women. But mostly her job was to be at home, in the kitchen, cooking, sewing, making jam, bread, and pies and, unfortunately, hamburgers like hockey pucks. It didn't seem an exciting life to me, one I had no interest in imitating.

World peace was one of the biggest things my parents had in common, but even more, the two of them loved classical music. They played violin and piano duets, went out to concerts, listened to records. They often talked about where they met, at a Chopin concert in England during the war. On their first date, Dad had borrowed a record player and they'd listened to late Beethoven string quartets. That music always made them sentimental. I liked classical music too, a bit, though I'd never admit it to them or especially to any of my friends, did not want to be square. But listening to Bach on the record player, or to *Romeo and Juliet* by that Russian composer, made me feel light and full. I'd leap and twirl around the living room in my ballet shoes.

Mr. Gagarin was Russian, like that composer. There was a Cold War going on, and Russians were the enemy. People were building fallout shelters in their basements, and my cousins in Washington were learning how to duck under their desks in case the Russians tried to wipe them out with a nuclear bomb. Everyone was very suspicious of Russians. Yet here was one standing on the green shores of the Northumberland Strait, a short, sweet man who let me wear his hat. Who could be afraid of Yuri Gagarin? Why did people need a war, even a cold one?

My father was saying life had not been easy for him and his left-wing friends. He and Cyrus Eaton, the rich man who'd sponsored this event, talked about how bad things were for people like them in the United States, how when they were visiting down there, they were sure they were tailed by the

FBI. It was the first time Daddy had mentioned this. Would the FBI come to arrest him?

Then I was glad my mother was different, not noisy and visible, of no interest to the FBI. In fact, she was quiet and almost invisible outside the house, though not inside. That was her English style; you should not be forward, you should never show off. Then why did she marry a man who shoved himself forward and showed off at every opportunity? Why did he marry a woman who disapproved of behaving that way? How confusing they were.

My mother was beautiful, and she loved men, all men, and they loved her. My grandmother used to laugh about her daughter's "come hither look." She told me about riding a London bus with Mum during the war, how a young man sitting opposite was so mesmerized by young Sylvia, he'd followed them off the bus and all the way home and had to be turned away.

But now Mummy was Mrs. Gordin Kaplan. My father was an Assistant Professor and the President of the Faculty Club and of various biological associations; he was always making speeches and writing articles and had his own program on local television, debating controversial issues. My mother took pottery and cello lessons and cared for us. When she was feeling unhappy, she'd tell me all over again that the stupidest thing she'd ever done was to leave school at the age of seventeen at the beginning of the war, to join the Land Army in Britain. "Don't ever leave school without a degree, Beth," she'd moan. "Otherwise you'll be left high and dry."

Did high and dry mean living in a nice house with a nice family? When we were in England, she did get a certificate in social work from the London School of Economics, and back in Halifax, she found a job as an apprentice social worker. Her first client was a woman with two young children whose husband beat her.

"Her story was so terrible," she told me, "I felt so sorry for her that I had to run into the bathroom to cry. I was a ghastly mess."

She never went back.

Well, maybe, I thought, *when you're beautiful and can get everyone to come hither, you don't have to go out to work.* She'd said my father was her investment.

Almost none of the other mothers we knew had jobs either. The men were out making a living, and the women were at home making nice things to eat, always there when the kids got home from school. The only women we knew who'd never been married, lived alone, and had jobs were Marie, a speech therapist, and Jean, a secretary. They weren't either of them pretty, probably couldn't find a man to marry them.

My mother had no admiration or respect for the women scientists Daddy worked with. She'd tell me how unhappy their husbands and children must be, how working women had to rely on uneducated maids to raise their kids and get meals on the table, because they were off selfishly pursuing their own careers, their own goals. I was glad Mum was at home with us and not off selfishly pursuing her own goals, whatever those might be.

I wondered if Yuri Gagarin had a wife, and if so, what she thought about his work, being hurled into space. Looking up at the sky to see where her husband was today.

****

Most of my friends at Tower Road School were already Brownies — Linda, Carol, Louise and Daphne, Kathy, Margie, Gillian. These were the girls in my class who went with their parents to church on Sundays and lived, I was sure, tidy, orderly lives. I wanted to go to Brownies too.

But Brownie meetings were held in a church basement. My dad didn't like churches, and he didn't think much of Brownies either.

"What the hell do you want her to do that regimented nonsense for?" he said to Mum. "March, salute, all that authoritarian crap."

"It teaches useful skills," my mother replied, "and she'll be with her friends."

I stood watching the battle between the giant He and She of my life. It made me nervous when my parents argued, and they argued a lot. But this time he shrugged, and she won. We went to buy the chocolate brown uniform, the beret, and the sash, and in September, with some of my Christian friends, I went to Brownies. Now I would learn to be like them. Like Linda, queen of the in crowd, whose mother, the one time Linda invited me to visit, had baked a lemon cake for an after-school snack, iced and everything. It was calm at Linda's. Her mother was not practicing the cello or sculpting in clay or going to meetings to save the planet from Strontium-90 and nuclear annihilation.

The church basement smelled of cleaning chemicals. All of us new girls — Tweenies — sat on the floor around a papier-mâché mushroom, the Magic Toadstool, while a tall woman with short brown hair, big teeth, and a blue uniform with a whistle told us that the Tweenies' first job was to learn the Brownie motto "Lend a Hand." She recited the Brownie Promise that we would all learn too:

I promise to do my best,
To do my duty,
To God, the Queen and my country,
To help other people every day,
Especially those at home.

The tall lady was familiar. She was the children's librarian at the Halifax Public Library where I went on Saturday afternoons, browsing through the dusty shelves and piling up books. She would stamp them loudly and warn me to bring them back on time, which I sometimes forgot to do. She always looked disapproving. Perhaps she would be nicer here. She told us to call her Brown Owl. There were other owls, Tawny Owl and Snowy Owl, with friendly smiles.

We sang songs and played games and learned how to earn badges and how to chant "tu whit, tu whit, tu whoo." At home, I told my father it was fun. He said, "My daughter, the Brownshirt."

"It's not a shirt," I said. "It's a dress."

After I'd joined the Pixie Sixes, it was time to begin work on badges. The Reading badge was the first one I got, easily — I could not live without reading — and then the Writing badge, which was the prettiest, with a quill pen. Then I got stuck. None of the other badges interested me much. The Housekeeping badge meant ironing a lot of different kinds of cloth. I didn't get around to all of them, but Mum wrote a note saying I had, so I'd get the badge. Mum loved badges.

My mother didn't read. "I don't have time," she said. "How do you have the patience to just sit there?" But she was good at everything to do with housekeeping — cooking, gardening, sewing, knitting, ironing. "Here, I'll help you," she'd say, with that eager voice. "What do we need to do?" My Baking badge did not go well; she ended up doing most of the recipes. And I loathed sewing. Not even my mother's persistent efforts could get me through the hemstitch.

One day, Brown Owl told us it was time to learn semaphore. "Semaphore is a language of flags," she said. "The combination and position of the flags make letters. When boating people are in trouble or need to communicate with each other across water, they use semaphore." This was especially necessary for us to learn, she added, since so many people in Halifax had sailboats.

My family did not own a sailboat, and we did not know how to sail. Dad had once applied to get us a membership at the Waegwoltic Club, where all my Brownie friends spent the summer holidays learning to swim and play tennis and sail, and where their families kept their boats. Dad was told we would not be permitted to join, that Jews were not allowed.

It didn't make sense. What was wrong with us? Dad said it was because of anti-Semitism, that people have always hated and excluded Jews. But why? Wasn't my family just as nice as Gillian's and Kathy's and Linda's? And in any case, my mother wasn't Jewish, so officially, according to Jewish law, I wasn't either. But there would be no Waeg for us.

I did not want to learn semaphore. First, my family was never going to sail. Second, if a boat was sinking, would the people on it really get out little coloured flags and wave them around? Wouldn't they scream "Help!" and jump up and down waving their arms instead?

Brown Owl handed out flags to the Sixers so they could begin to teach us semaphore. The girls started to move.

"Excuse me, Brown Owl," I said. "I wonder if I could learn something else."

Her eyes were little dark pellets. "Something else?" she said. "This is a pack. We do things together."

"I don't think semaphore will be a useful skill for me," I said. The girls froze. Brown Owl's face tightened.

"You will learn what the others learn, Elizabeth," she said. "Or else you will go home."

We learned A, B, C, and D, holding the flags at various angles in the right hand, and E, F, G, and H, held in the left. Just as we started the two flag letters, where you really needed to concentrate, the meeting was over. Tawny Owl came over to give me a special pat, but when we did our final "Tu whit, tu whit, tu whoo" in the circle, Brown Owl did not look at me.

At home, I said, "I'm thinking of quitting Brownies." Dad looked up over his newspaper and grinned. My mother was upset and wanted to know why, as we were only halfway through our Gardening badge.

When she saw I really did not want to go back, Mum set up a meeting with Brown Owl, to find out what had happened. At the library, we were taken to her little office at the back, where she sat in ordinary clothes behind a messy desk.

"Elizabeth is bright, Mrs. Kaplan," Brown Owl said, "capable, but wilful. She insists on her own way and does not conform to group discipline, which is essential."

My mother argued, trying to convince her to keep me in — She's younger than the others, things are difficult at home — but Brown Owl and I both knew our time together was over. Looking me right in the eyes, yet talking as if I were not in the room, she said, "Elizabeth had better beware. She's clever and quick, but many things in life require more than speed and cleverness. Unless she learns how to do the hard things and do them well, she'll be cursed all her life with a surface brilliance."

As we walked out, my mother bristled, "Your father has won again."

But I knew who had won. I knew Brown Owl's curse was seared into my skin, where no one would ever see it but me.

CORRESPONDENCE

t's time to revisit Barbara. The thought hit me as if winging through the frost-covered window, a voice ordering me to dig out Barbara's letters, see what was there.

Barbara, my childhood pen pal, died in June 1966, at the age of sixteen. It was now February 11, 2008, so her letters had been with me for nearly forty-two years. From my own sixteenth birthday a few months after her death, through university, career, marriage, children, and divorce, I'd safeguarded our four-year correspondence. And now, this cold morning, I obeyed the voice and tugged the black Ikea storage box from under the bed.

Beneath many papery mementoes, I dug out the plastic bag that held a jumble of thin blue aerograms and torn white envelopes — Barbara's letters. Just looking at her tidy green handwriting made my breath hurt. With the bag in my lap, I closed my eyes and tried to bring back the last time I'd seen my friend.

All that surfaced was a static black-and-white image from the one photograph she'd sent — tiny Barbara in a long white dress, a bridesmaid at a wedding. No animated face, no movement, no voice.

This was the mystery of Barbara. She was twelve and I was eleven in 1962 when our letters began to fly across the Atlantic, from her home in Wimbledon, outside of London, to mine in Halifax, Nova Scotia. In mid-1964, my family sailed from Halifax to live for a year in France, and on the way, we stopped to visit my British grandparents in London. One afternoon, my grandfather drove me in his minuscule old Morris, on the wrong side of the road, to have tea with my pen pal in Wimbledon.

The following summer, when we came through London on the way back to Halifax, I visited Barbara again, this time in hospital. Our two encounters are mentioned in her subsequent letters to me. Yet only a few years after her death, I could recall not a single detail of either visit — how she looked or sounded, her home and family, the hospital. Why had my mind chosen to erase all memory of Barbara? And not just my mind — there is no mention of these visits in my diaries, the diaries in which I chronicled everything that happened throughout my adolescence.

Almost everything.

****

"Here," said a girl at school, handing me a fistful of tattered envelopes. "You like writing — pick someone." She'd asked a British children's newspaper for a pen pal and was flooded with replies.

My choice was Barbara from Wimbledon, who sounded like a kindred spirit. "Please don't think me a square because I like classical music," she wrote, "as I like 'Pop' records too." So did I. Barbara loved ballet, animals, and dolls, and she collected stamps "in spasams." So did I.

After supper, I opened the box of special writing paper without lines. "I have a few foreign dolls," I wrote, "Korean, Italian and Americanian. We only have two animals at the moment: a one year old dachshund and my eight year old brother."

Within days, it seemed, the mailman brought a blue aerogram back to me; my new pal was keen to get started. To and fro our missives sailed. Both of us were avid readers and writers, but mostly, we were mad about ballet. *"Toe-shoes are painful,"* I informed her, *"but when you get used to being on toe, they feel and look beautiful!"*

Barbara revered everything about ballet, but although her younger sister Penny was taking classes, she was not. *"I don't do any dancing or any games or sport,"* she finally explained, *"though I would like to. In 1960 I had an operation for a 'hole in the heart' with which I was born but it was not discovered till I was ten.*

"It is not nearly so bad as it sounds, with nowadays all these wonderful discoveries of medicine. I am still not fully well yet, as I have to take medicines each day.

"A few nights ago I saw Margot Fonteyn and Rondulf Neurefv (spelling?) dance on television. They danced beautifully."

I didn't know what having a hole in your heart meant, except that my pen friend could not dance and was very small. Barbara was four foot three and wore a size two shoe. *"You make me feel quite a shrimp,"* she wrote cheerfully, *"because, although I am 14 weeks older than you, I am 9 ½ inches smaller."* She asked me to call her Babs.

Chatty Babs sent a relentless stream of letters, detailing the mishaps of little Penny and three older siblings. Her ambition was to go to art school like her brother Peter, and she often included skilful drawings, including a meticulous map of the bedroom she shared with Penny and many dolls. In return, I confided in her about my secret world, an island where I was a kind, beautiful orphan with waist-length blonde hair who rode her golden palomino bareback.

But in January 1964, aged thirteen and a half, I heard "She Loves You" on the hit parade and turned instantly into a Beatlemaniac. Fantasy islands, ballet, homework, anything other than my idols held no further interest. Lucky Barbara was right there, at the epicentre of Beatledom. *"Please, please send photos,"* I begged. *"Especially Paul."*

How proud I was at school, showing off the neatly clipped pictures direct from England. Although my new friend also liked the Beatles, John especially, she didn't adore them the way I did. *"I hope you don't mind me saying this,"* she wrote in her favourite green ink, *"but I think Ringo isn't very handsome. He's got such a large mouth and funny nose."*

Secretly I didn't think much of Ringo either, but no one, no one, criticized the best group in the universe. Despite my gratefulness for the precious clippings stuffed into her envelopes, I began to find Barbara's tales of ballerinas, kittens, and family pranks a bit babyish. At the same time, she often delivered stern lectures about the delay in my replies, sounding annoyingly bossy, like my annoyingly bossy British mother.

"What I do," Babs advised, *"is write MY letters as soon as I've received yours. Then I don't keep putting it off until I forget. I also try to mail them as soon as possible. Don't you agree?"*

That spring, there was exciting news to send to Wimbledon: for Dad's work, my family would be living for a year in a suburb of Paris. *"If we travel through London,"* I wrote, *"YOU AND I CAN MEET! A pen pal's dream."*

And we did meet, twice. Apparently.

During that tumultuous year, overwhelmed and lonely at an all-girl French high school, I kept myself company by writing stories and in my diary. On holidays, as my family camped around Europe, I sat in the backseat of our Peugeot, weaving long romantic tales about my life as Mrs. Paul McCartney to send to Beatle-mad friends at home. This left little time for writing to Babs. My pen friend was now confined to hospital; all she could offer were anecdotes about the nurses, with sketches of their old-fashioned uniforms and starched white caps. In return for every two of her letters, I managed a short reply or a breezy postcard.

On our journey home, I scribbled rapturously in my journal about seeing the Fab Four on my grandparents' television in London; about our day in sacred, magical Liverpool.

No mention, I noticed much later, of seeing my pen pal.

Home in Halifax in September 1965, I went to a high school with real boys and hurtled daily into love and out again. Babs remained in hospital, but the following spring, she sent an astonishing announcement: she'd been accepted at the world-famous Mayo Clinic for an operation to repair her heart. She and her mother would fly to Rochester, Minnesota, in June. I was thrilled to imagine her healthy and strong, going to dances, falling in love, married with babies. As surely I would be, soon.

I picked up my pen.

"As usual, Babs, I must say 'Sorry not to have written in so long.' You must excuse me – school is terribly hard."

She'd asked me to glean information from my scientist dad about the Mayo Clinic. "He says it's the best place in the world for such an operation," my letter continued, with pages of Dad's reassuring details about the town, the clinic, and her surgeon, and including two American dollars Dad passed on for her.

In May 1966, just after her sixteenth birthday, Barbara wrote from hospital, "Thank you so much for the letter and the $2. It was very kind and thoughtful of you.

"I'm madly excited, everyone is trying to 'sit' on me to keep me quiet but it's no good. Please do write while I'm there."

The address in Minnesota was on my desk, because she'd sent it in two previous letters. But I was preoccupied — exams, first boyfriend, first kiss — and did not write it on an envelope.

In late June, I was alone in the house, dancing to "Rubber Soul," when the mail dropped through the front door. I saw the familiar blue of an aerogram and with a jolt, remembered Barbara's operation. Here she was, to tell me all about it.

But the careful round handwriting was not hers. The return address showed the name of her mother, Elsie, in Wimbledon. My throat clenched.

"Beth, I am writing to tell you that Barbara had her operation in America on June 9th. They mended the hole and put two plastic valves in. I am very sorry to have to tell you that Barbara passed away from us on June 15th.

"Thank you for being such a special friend."

All day, I held the letter tight. How could she be dead, dead at barely sixteen? And I healthy and alive? Eyes raw, cheeks wet and burning, I gathered together my pen friend's letters. But as I sat on my bedroom floor unfolding them, instead of the usual companionship of her voice came a series of excruciating blows.

"Please, please, a million times, will you write to me? I look forward to your letters immensely especially when I'm in hospital," I read, and in the next missive, and the next, more entreaties.

"I've been waiting for the letter I haven't yet received!!!!!!!! Maybe you've been too busy to write though. Never mind, maybe you will now."

While my friend lay in hospital struggling to breathe, I was touring Europe, absorbed in dreams. I'd never really thought about her, unable to walk out into the sun, let alone travel the world. Why hadn't it occurred to me to share my experiences with Babs, bring the world to her in letters? I bent over in agony, to imagine my ill friend waiting for the words that rarely came.

What I had done — no, what I had not done — was unforgivable. I could never tell her how sorry I was, never make it right. Guilt engulfed me. Sobbing in my room, the walls still covered with Beatle pictures sent from Wimbledon, I swore to use my love of writing to keep not just myself but the world company. No one would complain, ever again, about not hearing from me.

That Christmas, I wrote to Barbara's family. Her mother Elsie sent back a sweet, mournful note, describing all that had gone wrong in their time at the Mayo and inviting me to visit. Though only five years later I attended theatre school in London, Elsie's invitation, my bond with the family, the proximity of London to Wimbledon, were forgotten.

****

While rereading Barbara's letters, I wondered if Elsie was still going strong, like my own old but formidable mother. If so, I could tell her how much her daughter had always meant to me; that I'd become a writer partially thanks to Babs. Would it be possible, through the miracle of the Internet, to touch my pen friend again, make sense of the loss of her? I Googled Elsie without success, and Penny. They'd vanished.

Then I remembered Barbara's older brother Peter, and after a search, there he was, a graphic artist with an address in London. I wrote him a letter explaining my purpose for writing. No reply, for weeks.

One morning, in my email in-box:

Subject: Barbara.
From: Penny.

Babs's little sister remembered meeting me in Wimbledon in 1964. I'd signed her autograph book, "From Beth, an uncurable Beatlemaniac."

"Barbara touched the lives of many but you were a special friend. You gave her a taste of the teenage life she was never able to experience. You described the Mayo Clinic in a way that inspired confidence and excitement. Our thanks to you for that.

"I remember so little of my sister, although she's with me all the time."

Elsie had died only recently, I was sorry to learn, but Penny and I began to correspond. She too was an ardent letter writer and chronicler, and we became immediate online friends. I photocopied Barbara's letters — ninety dense pages — to send to England. Though Penny had been concerned what her sister might reveal about the family, "Babs was more than kind," she wrote me, "and I was overjoyed to hear her voice again."

"It's tragic Mum just missed meeting you again, Beth," Penny emailed a few days later. "She died barely a week before your letter came. That's why Peter delayed showing us your note – because the timing was so odd."

My heart lurched.

"Penny, what was the exact date of your mother's death?" I wrote.

"The 11th of February 2008," replied Penny. "Why?"

What it means I don't know, but after storing Barbara's letters for more than four decades, the day I felt compelled to pull them out and begin the search for her was the day her mother died.

Penny was sure my letters to Wimbledon had long been discarded. But one evening, celebrating her birthday with her two grown children, she was rifling through an old box of family photographs when she discovered a hidden packet — my letters, all my letters to Barbara. They'd opened and read.

"Babs was buried exactly 42 years ago on my 11th birthday, Beth, and I've been trying to break the spell ever since," she wrote. "Your letters brought my sister to life. We talked for hours about Babs, how my children grew up seeing her picture on the wall but never liking to ask about her. We broke the spell by laughing so much at your letters.

"You have allowed me both to celebrate my lost sister and to confront the grief bottled up for so long. I lost my mother but found my sister's friend and I think that is more than a coincidence. It is a blessing."

A week later, the letter carrier deposited a small parcel from England in my mailbox. Inside was a brown paper bag, once taped shut, with Barbara's neat green writing on the front: *Beth's Letters To Me.*

And so I met again my teenaged self, lovelorn, melodramatic, besieged. As expected, my notes were not as frequent as Barbara's. But to my surprise I did write fairly often, sometimes a long, newsy, funny letter. I did send her gifts, as she did to me. Flawed as her correspondent had been, my friend, before flying off to her last chance at life, had tucked the letters in a secret place, to be reclaimed on her return. I'd grown up haunted by my neglect of a friend in need. But perhaps she'd been given something of value, after all.

"*We all live with regret and guilt,*" wrote Penny once. "*None of us had done enough.*"

Sitting with my own letters in my lap, I thought about the Barbara-sized hole in my memory. Visiting my pen pal, I'd expected to encounter the sunny, robust writer I knew through the mail. But Penny had told me how wan and fragile her sister was by the time we met, her skin almost transparent. In hospital, Penny said, Babs had worn a wig she was proud of, poufy with a fashionable flip, which looked odd atop her thin white face.

Perhaps it was a shock for my teenaged self, already in turmoil, to witness such heartrending frailty in a friend the same age. Perhaps I couldn't bear to acknowledge her vulnerability and terrible blind need. Easier, wiser even, to close the door to memory and move on.

The following year, after much emailing, I flew to England to stay with Penny. She'd organized a weeklong visit for us, a risky venture for two middle-aged women who'd met for only five minutes in childhood. But immediately we felt like family, chatting long into the night, poring over her mementos and archives, dancing to the Beatles. She described her mother's journey back from Minnesota, alone, accompanied by a small white coffin. We talked about the lifelong effects of Barbara's death, the weight of remorse and sorrow carried for so long, and rage, too, that this girl did not have a chance at life.

As my new pen pal and I sat laughing and weeping, black-and-white photos spread before us, we both knew she was there too. Our sister, our friend, the lightest and most tenacious of ghosts.

"Do you think we'll be friends forever, Babs?" I wrote in what turned out to be my last letter. Her answer came instantly, as her answers always did.

"Of course we will, silly," she said. "I feel I've known you all my life and I've grown up with you. BethandBabs Forever!

All my love,
Barbara.

P.S. Please please please please write."

And I do.

Postscripts for Looking Back:

On the road again: In 1995, fifteen years after quitting the theatre, I was asked to go back onstage in Vancouver, to play a lead role in a highbrow American comedy. Our kind babysitter offered to move into the house with the kids, so I flew to the west coast, determined that this time, at forty-five, I would triumph at this job. After all the therapy, I felt strong emotionally, and was physically fit because of the Y. I even brought some party clothes, thinking of the stage door johnnies who'd line up to take this new star dancing.

The experience nearly killed me. The moment rehearsals began, my insecurities sprang to the fore, and with good reason: one of the other leads was determined to upstage my every move, the production was underfunded and majorly under-rehearsed, and on opening night, I had bronchitis so severe, I could hardly speak and had to take steroids to get through. My exhausted body dropped over ten pounds in two months. I crawled home after every show.

And yet, night after night, more of what was required on that stage came clear, as I figured out how to bring another human being to life, to inhabit and illuminate her soul as truthfully and with as much depth as possible while still soliciting laughs. By closing night, I felt I'd finally grasped the role and made it mine. As the final lights went down on me singing a song to the daughter in my arms, a woman in the front row sighed loudly with pleasure.

"Just perfect!" she exclaimed.

And then, applause fading, we actors finishing our bows, she turned to her companions.

"Now," she said briskly, "where shall we go for dinner?"

L'Arche: I asked Lynn that summer of 1979 about Jean Vanier's sexuality; he was not a priest so could marry but had no evident liasons. She replied that he was a deeply spiritual man, perhaps asexual, who seemed to have no need for a partner.

After Vanier's death, L'Arche launched an investigation and uncovered the appalling truth that, in the guise of spiritual communion, Vanier had sexually abused at least twenty-five female assistants, including nuns. The news was devastating; the man was considered a saint, and there'd been talk he would be canonized. The sense of betrayal was incalculable.

In retrospect, it's clear troubling issues of sexuality were never dealt with in the early days of L'Arche but, in true Catholic tradition, were shoved under the carpet. I find it difficult to comprehend a religion that continues to be criminally repressive about normal human biological impulses and necessities, resulting in centuries of immense anguish and harm. Just ask the Indigenous peoples of Canada.

But no matter what the sins of its founder and his religion, nothing will take away the immense good L'Arche has done and continues to do in hundreds of communities around the world.

My experience there meant so much to me that I wrote a memoir, Loose Woman: my odyssey from lost to found, *about it.*

1961: *"Orbiting Earth in the spaceship, I saw how beautiful our planet is. People, let us preserve and increase this beauty, not destroy it!"*

Russian cosmonaut Yuri Gagarin, first human in space (1934-1968)

Correspondence: *Penny and I still write and, despite living on different continents, have managed to visit each other every so often. After countless drafts, the essay about Barbara was published in a literary magazine, with photographs of Barbara's letters and mine, and of Barbara herself. I sent it proudly to Penny to share with her siblings: their sister memorialized and honoured.*

But Penny was horrified. In the essay, I quoted her as saying the wig Babs wore in hospital looked "absurd" atop her thin white face. That was what I remembered.

"I thought the wig looked beautiful!" she protested. "I would never say something so hurtful, that it looked absurd."

One word out of the thousands was clumsy and misguided and had done harm. I changed "absurd" to "odd" and apologized profusely.

Another of the dilemmas for the writer of true stories: those we write about have memories and opinions too.

These essays appeared in:

Groupie, *Globe and Mail*, 1998
"On the Road Again," *Fresh Air*, CBC, 1998
"L'Arche," *This Morning*, CBC, 1997
Correspondence, *Queen's Quarterly*, 2022

CRAZYTIME

If you have no wounds how can you know if you're alive?
If you have no scar how do you know who you are?

Edward Albee

WINE GLASS, HALF FULL

went to my first Alcoholics Anonymous meeting last night.

Not as a confirmed alcoholic, no, but as a visitor. My friend Ted, whom I met at the Y, has spoken so often about his evenings at AA that I wanted to see what goes on there. Well, okay, I did have a little concern about my own drinking. Ted gave me the AA list of questions that determines whether you're an alcoholic or not, and I'd answered an emphatic "yes" to two of them: "Do you drink alone?" and "Do you crave a drink at a definite time daily?"

I live with two teenagers so yes, I drink wine by myself, and yes, at five o'clock I am more than ready for my generous first glass, followed by one or two more. According to the brochure, that meant I was possibly, but not necessarily, an alcoholic. So I went with Ted.

My friend is a loud, gregarious guy with a heart of gold and a ton of problems, which he happily acknowledges. Ted spent his twenties as a womanizing, alcoholic, drug-addicted West Coast logger, and barely lived to tell the tales; mesmerizing tales they are, too. One drunk and disorderly weekend, for example, Ted was so attentive to a woman in a bar that her boyfriend chased him out into the street. Ted ran straight into a '66 Beaumont, smashed through its windshield and dented its roof before being hauled off to hospital. There he was so noisy and disruptive that they bandaged him, gave him Demerol — "Mmm, Demerol," he says fondly — and pushed him out the door. He rented a car, drank, did drugs, smacked into a tree, and landed back in hospital. That was one weekend.

Eventually, Ted ended up unemployed in Toronto, huddled in a dark room, an alcoholic junkie. Instead of dying, he went to an AA meeting and stopped drinking and drugs, cold turkey. Ten years ago, this summer.

As we drove to the meeting, I thought about my friend's harsh childhood, his vicious stepfather who was an alcoholic himself. "My stepfather couldn't get sober," Ted told me one day, matter-of-factly. "He hung himself. I found him." He'd mentioned other appalling events from his past. I wondered how he dulls the pain now.

That's what the glass of booze is for, isn't it? Not the goblet of wine to accompany the filet, or the flute of champagne at New Year's, but the glass you keep filling and emptying, over and over again. People don't keep getting drunk out of greed, or curiosity. Isn't it because something hurts in some hole inside, and a boozy oblivion might take away the pain for a while? But, hole or not, most of us eventually listen to the voice that says, "That's enough. Stop now."

Ted had no such voice. Like many alcoholics, he says, "One drink is too many, and a thousand are not enough."

As we pulled up to the church hall at the end of a street lined with mansions, I asked how he has kept going without numbing drugs.

"I pray to a higher power," he answered, "and I go right through it. I face the pain."

The brightly lit room was packed. A man in a cashmere overcoat, who looked as if he'd just stepped from the corporate jet, sat next to a man in a ski jacket who might just have got out of jail. Women who looked like hookers, and models, and model housewives, and schoolgirls, and the girl next door. Men like bouncers and insurance executives and gold-medal-winning snowboarders. A hundred people, sitting in rows, with nothing in common except alcoholism — and thus, a lifelong bond.

A solid middle-aged woman rose to chair the meeting. "Hi, my name is Cindy and I'm an alcoholic," she said. Everyone chorused, "Hi Cindy!" The main business of the night was to award a chip to Jennifer, who'd gone a year without a drink. Various members rose to speak in praise. Jennifer, a pretty young blonde whose parents sat beside her, spoke of the loneliness and desperation of the years lost to the bottle. And now, a roomful of supporters, her smiling parents, a chip.

The chair then called up those who'd gone six months without a drink, three months, one month. "And who has the desire to quit drinking today?" she asked. A man stood up to applause and cheers; he'd recently fallen off the wagon, after seven years of sobriety.

"Keep coming back," was one of the slogans on a billboard at the front of the stage. "One day at a time."

The speakers were moving and honest, each with a tale of turning to face the monster. I learned the battle never ends. There was cake after the meeting, but Ted didn't have any. He can't eat chocolate, or drink coffee; for him, even caffeine is a "mood-altering substance." He used to go to fourteen

AA meetings a week; now he's down to two or three. A lot of his spare time goes into helping others with their alcohol and drug problems.

"AA is about saving yourself, and then serving others," he told me. Soon, Ted will get his ten-year chip. "Remember when," said the sign on the stage.

I was warmed by the compassion and optimism in that room, by the power of the human need for community. But it was a relief to realize I won't need to return. I do like and need my wine at five sharp, and definitely drink more than is healthy alone. Someday I'll fix that. But at the meeting, I understood the difference between AA members and me: I can, in fact, take the wine, or leave it. Coffee would be nearly impossible to live without, but wine, no. If forced to give up my five o'clock ritual, I'd miss it a great deal but could do so. My life has given me another set of compulsions, a different way of coping.

Despite my many problems and flaws, it's a relief to know alcoholism is not on the long list of things to fret about.

The last message on the billboard was for me. "There but for the grace of God," it said.

STRANGER ON A TRAIN

I tried to have a romantic adventure this summer; I really did. The setting couldn't have been more conducive: the night train from Venice to Paris. My compartment on the way in to Venice was crammed with strangers, but on the way out, there was only me, blissfully alone. I was relishing the privacy and quiet when a man poked his head in and asked if he could join me.

He was good-looking and fit, with grizzled curls and an intense gaze — Italian, fluent in English. We began to chat. He was witty, magnetic, and without a wedding ring, and a Harlequin fantasy began to unfurl in my mind — "Strangers in the Night." Our eyes locked, the conversation picked up heat, and we jumped into more personal matters. Soon I knew more than I could ever want to know about him, because we spent the next two hours discussing his divorce.

He couldn't stop talking about it, and try as I might, I couldn't steer the conversation away. His ex-wife's family always destroyed their men, he said; there wasn't a man left anywhere in her bunch. How would he keep the love of his four daughters when she was poisoning their thoughts? he asked me. I made empathetic noises, although divorce is not my preferred topic of discussion with a handsome stranger in the dead of night, with Italy flashing by outside the window.

In Milan, other passengers appeared. We all pulled down our beds and went to sleep, and in the morning my Italian friend, grasping my hand, thanked me profusely for listening and dashed off.

This was not an isolated incident. In the spring an old high-school buddy turned up; a skinny teenager with an Afro when we last met, now he's balding, with a paunch. Right away the saga emerged: he'd left his wife, which meant leaving his children too, and was still in the thick of turmoil and guilt. We sat in the garden, old friends meeting after three decades, going over and over — what else? — how to survive divorce. Then another old buddy called; same problem, same turmoil. Old girlfriends too; not long ago, a schoolmate's marriage ended, and she's consumed with rage, incomprehension, pain.

What's going on out there? Perhaps it's just my Boomer generation's self-centred, I-want-everything-right-now ethos. Whatever the reasons, unhappy husbands and wives don't know that, while separation ends the troubles of the marriage, it unleashes a breathtaking array of brand-new troubles. And that's just for the adults involved, let alone for the greatest victims, the children.

Divorce, almost any divorce, is a disaster for the soul. The wounded on both sides are left struggling to figure out what hit them, and why it hurts so much.

As I had to, once.

When my ex and I decided to separate, our intention was to make a clean break. What I immediately discovered is that, in a divorce with children, "clean break" is an oxymoron. I knew about the anguish of marriage. What now confronted me was the anguish of divorce: a split necessitated not by abuse, addiction, or violence of any kind, just a mundane breakup between two discontented people wanting the best for everyone involved.

Being a good parent is a tremendously time-consuming, demanding job, hard enough in a stable environment. How much more difficult when the job is divided between two households with different rules and expectations, sometimes headed (though not, I'm glad to say, in our case) by two people who can't stand to see or talk to each other and use the child as a pawn, or a go-between, or a crutch.

Add to this the nightmare of logistics, moving back and forth, the endless complications of Christmas, birthdays, school events, his new wife, her boyfriend, stepfamilies. Custodial parents almost always suffer a huge drop in income, which means little time, energy, or money to spare. Many single parents are debilitated by grief, loneliness, fear, anger, their children's struggles and pain.

The great heroes of our society, to me, are the solitary mothers and fathers who despite great difficulties do their best to parent with loving attentiveness. Their children will grow up knowing that marriage takes work, that loss and upheaval can be overcome. Countless other children of divorce, from all over the demographic map, will carry a bleaker message into adulthood.

Although the years after divorce remain in my mind a dark and tangled nightmare, I was immensely privileged in many ways. Support from my ex meant I could see a skilled therapist, an invaluable anchor of sanity and calm. When my children had problems dealing with the enormous changes in their lives, we saw a family counsellor, who asked once to see the children's father too. At one point I had three different weekly therapeutic commitments, including a single parent's support group. Trying to fix us was a part-time job.

It was worth it.

Years later, I know why the split was unavoidable and necessary, at least for me. As Doris the butcher's wife pointed out, I did what I had to do to become who I have become. Who I am.

And yet the divorce remains the greatest tragedy of my life — because it meant the end of promise and hope and love; because he and I produced two human beings together, the greatest act of intimacy and creativity possible, and now the parents of those children know very little about each other. The end of my marriage, although it was mutually agreed upon, and though he and I have at last regained something of a friendship, left a grief that was acute for years, is still there, and will always be there.

I regretted my non-romance on the train but understood my Italian fellow traveller. The wound was new, for him. Whether the separation is wanted or involuntary, a person leaving a long-term marriage, especially one with children, is a sudden amputee, dealing with the loss of a leg, an arm, an eye.

In one way, divorce is like marriage: you have no idea what it's going to be like until you're in the thick of it. But at least marriage usually provides some pleasure and companionship before it goes wrong. The only good thing to say about the demise of a marital union is that sometimes it's not too hideous, and you get used to it. And sometimes, in the end, it turns out to be healthy. Sometimes life without that partner is better, in the end.

But when divorce is new — even when you're in the world's most beautiful country, communing with a sympathetic stranger on a velvet August night — it will be sitting there, too, right next to you, hanging on every word.

SECRET

enny Harris, my special childhood friend, remained invisible. For more than two decades, I'd been looking for her, periodically Googling both her name and the various ways her workplace might come up, without success. And then last week, one of those ideas that spark through the air struck me: although neither of us had ever used her full name back then, I should try it now. Penelope.

In an instant, there she was: Penelope Jane Harris. It was her obituary. She'd died the year before. I was too late.

The memory of the last time we'd met would never leave me.

"Name's Penny," she said. "What's yours?"

Penny wore thick-framed glasses, her straight black hair cut in a pudding bowl, pale skin erupting into angry patches of red. We were at a neighbourhood birthday party where neither of us, both weird outsiders, knew why we'd been invited. While the in-crowd girls in their frilly dresses gossiped and giggled and played Pin the Tail on the Donkey in the den, Penny and I sat on the turquoise brocade sofa in the living room swooning over our favourite book, *Little Women*. She preferred intrepid Jo, and I my namesake, saintly Beth. I told Penny I wept for days after reading the tragic chapter where Beth says goodbye to Jo and then dies with the sun shining on her sweet face.

Penny's head drooped. She touched her eye, then leaned over and smeared a wet finger down my cheek.

"Real tears," she whispered.

Wow. She's weirder than I am, I thought, touching the damp on my face, *and she doesn't care.*

We were soulmates.

This was Halifax in 1962. She was thirteen. I was eleven.

My new best friend lived in a child's drawing kind of house, a white box with a pointy roof, in the middle a black front door with black-shuttered windows on either side. The windows were always closed, the downstairs rooms spotless and airless. Penny's dad was tall and hurried, like the White Rabbit in *Alice in Wonderland*; when Penny introduced us, he bent quickly to shake my fingertips and vanished. Her mother was short and wiry with sharp eyes and a sharp voice. She was always tired, never offered Kool-Aid and cookies like mothers were supposed to. It was clear she wasn't keen on me, Penny's only good friend, coming over to play, but she never allowed her daughter to visit my house, I didn't know why. She ordered us to keep quiet. *Quiet!*

We tiptoed to Penny's room and closed the door. Playing outside, even in the backyard, was not an option; my friend was always wheezing with allergies and asthma. She also had eczema, scaly bumpy patches on her elbows and the backs of her knees that made her scratch until she bled, although she struggled not to. "My scratching," she whispered once, "makes Mum very angry."

We played with dolls, real ones and paper ones, while we talked about our schools and books and dreams. One day she wanted to tell me a secret.

"Guess what?" she murmured, pushing her glasses back up her nose, as she did constantly. "I was adopted."

I'd never met anyone who was adopted and wasn't sure how to respond. "That's neat," I said, holding the shapely new Barbie paper doll we'd been dressing. "Were … were you in an orphanage and everything?"

"Don't know," she said. "I heard my real mother had tons of children already and didn't have room for me."

"I hope you were in an orphanage, Pen," I said, thinking of Anne of Green Gables. "That's so romantic."

She turned away. "When I see a woman with lots of kids," she said, her finger tracing the bright paper dress in her lap, "I wonder if she's my mother. I wonder if she ever changed her mind."

I'd often imagined I was adopted. Surely my actual birth parents were nicer than the ones I was stuck with. But deep down I knew that was a fantasy, whereas, it shocked me to realize, Penny really did not know who her birth parents were.

I was a demonstrative girl and wanted to hug her, but sensed it best to keep my distance. We never touched.

Penny was excited to invite me one Saturday for lunch with her parents. We sat stiffly in the dining room around a large mahogany table, exchanging awkward remarks, while her mother served Campbell's tomato soup and Kraft cheese sandwiches, not quite enough for the four of us.

My family has lots of problems, I thought, *but coming up with food and conversation is not one of them.*

If they'd invited me back for a meal, I'd have found an excuse not to go. But an invitation never came again.

Penny and I were mad for figurines. When either of us had saved enough allowance, we'd get the bus downtown to Woolworth's on Barrington Street and buy a new figurine, small china horses mostly. We gave them names: Violin, Dancer, Fanfare. One day, playing stables in her room, we decided to create special homes for our horses out of whatever we could find. She sprawled on the floor on one side of her bed, and I on the other, in silence all afternoon, making up dramas.

For some time, our afternoons together were dedicated to creating miniature exhibitions that we called Project X. I would decide, say, on a hospital scene and make beds out of cardboard and Kleenex, an operating room of Plasticine and matchboxes, a row of bandaged horses lined up, recovering. Wheezing on the other side, Penny was creating a fairy horse's treehouse of old cheesecloth dusters, bits of jewellery, wood scraps glued together.

And then we had the thrilling notion to create an entire new world; words and ideas tumbling out, we pieced the story together. I became Helen Foster and she Kristine Foster, orphan twins — fraternal, not identical — whose parents had died in a terrible fire. We'd been sent to stay with our curmudgeonly Aunt Gwendolyn on Foster Island, off the coast of England. In real life, I was sturdy with short brown hair, but my willowy Helen had blonde locks cascading to her waist and a delicate face and voice. Everyone loved Helen for her selfless kindness. Penny's Kristine was a fierce, reckless tomboy always charming her way out of scrapes. "She looks like me," said Penny, "only prettier."

Foster Island was mostly fields and woods, so we had our own horses. Mine, Champ, was a golden palomino. Kristine's Firefly was a pinto. We rode bareback.

Penny and I kept two diaries, one for Foster Island and one for our real lives. At home, I was miserably caught between my parents. My chubby little brother, with his blonde curls and dimples, was the adored favourite of them both, especially Dad, and the injustice of my exclusion from my father's heart burned in me. Dad intimated that girls who liked dolls and dresses were boring conformists. He wanted a rebellious tomboy, like my Foster Island sister Kristine.

But I was gentle Helen, and despite the pain caused me by others, I tried to forgive everyone and everything. "Helen," I wrote in my Beth diary, "is a kind of saint with an indescribable inner radiance." When my mother yelled to clean my room, or Dad smacked the side of my head for some misdemeanour, as he often did, I'd choke back tears and do my best to turn into Helen. In my room, looking around at the jumble, I'd murmur, "Oh, dear Kristine, look what a mess you've made! I'll clean it up for you." And humming softly, I sorted the clothes, tidied the papers, put away the stacks of books. How good it felt to be someone else, neat and serene and cherished.

With all my miseries, however, it was clear in the way Penny crept about her sealed home that her life was way worse than mine. Although she was an only child, her parents never seemed to hug her or even talk much to her. Sometimes when she opened the front door, I couldn't help but notice her swollen eyes. On those days, the white house felt darker than ever. But I pushed away any thoughts about my friend's difficulties; maybe the chilly remoteness in her home was normal and happened in other homes. In all our time together, Penny and I never discussed our family situations or our parents. I caught glimpses of her real-life diary, covered with her big black scrawl, but never saw what she wrote. We only discussed Foster Island — how we, brave sisters, could thwart foolish, crabby Aunt Gwendolyn to get what we wanted.

One afternoon, a new treat: Kristine and Helen discovered a perfect little house deep in the forest. We loved being on Foster Island, but the secret cottage was our favourite place. In my Helen diary, I drew a picture of it, hidden in the trees, with a thatched roof and bright sunny windows. There were matching hooked rugs in the bedroom, beside Kristine's bed and mine. Champ and Firefly grazed in the field of wildflowers outside the front door.

By the time Penny turned fourteen, she'd got a bra and her period and discovered pop music. "You don't listen to the hit parade?" she asked one day, and I boiled at the condescension in her voice. She began to spend her money not on figurines but on 45s, which she insisted on playing for me, snapping her fingers. I told her "Louie Louie" was the stupidest song I'd ever heard. "Twelve's too young to get it, I guess," she shrugged.

The change in my friend upset me. But still, most weekends, she and I sailed to our island and played there all day.

When Penny told me her father had taken a job in Victoria, on the other side of the country, we both cried real tears. But immediately, we turned our separation into a story. Kristine, we decided, was being sent to a special boarding school on the other side of the country, but her unfortunate twin couldn't go. Helen's faithful German shepherd had chased a rabbit onto the road, and she'd thrown herself in front of a car to save him. Legs crushed, she was now confined to a wheelchair. But she bore her disability with infinite patience.

Penny and I swore to write to each other forever, and for a while we did, one letter from friend to friend, and another, in the same envelope, from sister to sister. I wrote to Penny that school was a drag and my Hayley Mills scrapbook was filling up, and Helen told Kristine she was gaining strength in her legs; "I might even walk with crutches one day!" There were also notes in Aunt Gwendolyn's flowery script, hoping her far-away niece was doing her algebra homework and eating her lima beans.

Envelopes from my friend included scribbled missives to Aunt Gwendolyn from despairing teachers at Kristine's school, while Penny wrote about the actual boarding school her parents had sent her to, which she liked a lot and where she'd made a friend. And then came the day Penny sent only one letter. "I can't do Foster Island anymore," she wrote. "I'm too old for little kid crap."

For a minute, I couldn't breathe. I was not ready to be exiled. Just a bit longer, please, I wanted to beg.

A few days later, I carefully hand-printed and mailed an official-looking document. "To Miss Kristine Foster," it said. "We regret to inform you that Foster Island has been destroyed by a long dormant volcano. Everything on the island was buried except for a burned and twisted wheelchair. Please accept our sincerest apologies, and best wishes for your future."

Penny did not reply.

More than three decades later, I was hired by a Vancouver theatre to act in a play. A forty-five-year-old single mother, I was also a former actress attempting a comeback. One night, waiting for me at the stage door was a familiar form with dark pudding bowl hair, pale blotchy skin, and black-rimmed glasses. I knew her instantly. "Penny!" I exclaimed. "Real tears!"

We met for coffee, spilling over with fond reminiscences of Project X and Foster Island. I told her about the confused decade of my twenties, my marriage, divorce, children, and recent work as a writer. Despite all those vivid childhood fantasies, I said, I now write only nonfiction because true stories matter most to me. It has taken a long time and a lot of professional help, I said, but right now, life feels pretty good.

At forty-seven, Penny had never had a partner and had always lived alone, but she enjoyed her work hunting down tax cheats for Canada Revenue. "I think I might be gay," she said, looking sharply at me to see if I was shocked, "but I'm really not sure." I told her many of my artsy friends were gay, and I'd even explored once if I was too. Another bond.

Waiting until the waitress had refilled our coffee cups and left, my friend leaned closer and told me softly that her mother had recently died.

"After the funeral," she said, her face expressionless, "Dad finally apologized to me for what happened during my childhood."

As she took a breath to go on, I knew. I knew what she was going to say.

"There was something really wrong with Mum." Penny pushed her glasses back up her nose, her voice monotone. "I mean emotionally, mentally. She liked to torture me. My playtime with you was one of my only escapes."

My stomach heaved as my friend talked about years of anguish at the hands of her mother. "She locked me in the basement, sometimes I didn't even know why," she said, as I shook my head in horror. "She beat me and mocked me when I cried. Or it was just she wouldn't give me anything to eat. No dinner for you for a week, she'd say."

"Oh my God, Penny," I said.

"Before I met you, my parents adopted a little boy, Sean," she told me, chapped hands gripping her coffee cup. "He was the joy of my life. I'd run home from school to take care of him. Then one day, I got home and Sean was gone. Without a word of warning, my mother'd sent him back. She told me she couldn't cope with him," Penny said, "and if I wasn't careful, the same thing would happen to me."

I writhed in my seat, heartsick.

"I should have done something, helped in some way," I cried.

"Nobody knew what was going on, Beth," she said, so quietly it was hard to hear. "No one."

I made a move to hug my friend, to convey concern and care, but the prickly barrier surrounding her was as impenetrable as ever. Perhaps now, as then, I thought, admitting vulnerability, allowing in compassion, would hurt too much.

We pledged to renew our correspondence — not by email, but by real mail, like before — and after my return home, our letters began to flow again. Being in touch with a treasured childhood friend, reading her familiar black scrawl, gave me immense pleasure; something vital and long missing had been found. Though still anxious and hypersensitive, I was well on my way to feeling truly at home in the world. I hoped my friend was, too.

One day she wrote to say she had exciting news: she'd met a wonderful man and was madly in love. He was struggling financially, she said, with an unfair, demanding ex-wife and two children; last year, through no fault of his own, he'd lost his job. She had invited him to live at her place and would gladly support him until he got back on his feet. She was sure he'd soon find a job, and her life would be happier than it had ever been.

"Do you remember our secret cottage in the woods?" she wrote. "I feel like I live there now."

"Yikes, no, Penny," I said out loud. How could I not be concerned by what she'd described, her lonely susceptibility to what sounded like a manipulative man? Should I say something? I'd failed to help her a long time ago and must do so now. But how? Finally, thinking I might be the only person she trusted, wanting above all to protect her, I wrote a gentle letter, begging her to be careful with her heart.

I never heard from her again.

After all those years of wondering about my friend and trying to reach her, it made me weep to read the brevity of her obituary: Penelope Jane Harris, August 31 1948 - August 19 2019. There were no messages of condolence. I was desolate. If only just once I'd been able to offer an embrace, to express my love, my gratitude for her immense courage and imagination and her friendship.

And then, scrolling through the Internet, I discovered something else: a B.C. woman named Penelope Harris had donated two parcels of land to a local First Nation. Clicking further, I found a series of photographs. This Penelope Harris had very short white hair and no glasses. But she had my friend's cheekbones, her eyebrows. Her lively face.

Penny had bought two small parcels of land near Prince George as an investment; decades later, the area still undeveloped, she'd given the land to the Lheidli T'enneh First Nation. In April 2019, she travelled from her home in Abbotsford to Prince George for a ceremony during which they'd celebrated her generosity.

"I feel there is nothing we can do to fix all the things we've done wrong as a society to Canada's Aboriginal peoples," she said in a speech covered by the local press. "The line we were all fed about what the Canadian identity was, how great the Canadian story was, that has now fallen to pieces for all to see. Good. We were all duped. We've been lied to for generations. But we know that now.

"What are we doing now to make things right?"

In response, the chief called the gift "reconciliation in action."

"We will always think of Ms. Harris as one of us," he said.

Penny died four months later.

The First Nation community gave my friend a beautiful black and red hand-embroidered jacket. In the photos, she's wearing the ceremonial coat, and her face is radiant.

FIRE

stood on the sidewalk, watching my home burn. It was a perfect, placid August afternoon, the sky radiant, birds chittering, neighbours returning from work, parking cars, carrying groceries. From every window of my house, basement to attic, poured thick black smoke that blotted out the sun.

The howl of sirens. So often I'd heard that shriek and wondered whose crisis it signalled. Today it was mine. Gorgeous red machines wailed the wrong way up our one-way street — one, two, three giant gleaming pumpers, lights flashing, parking helter-skelter in the middle of the road, up over the curb. Big men leapt from the sides, grabbing helmets, overalls, boots, axes. I ran over to blurt out what happened — *basement, sauna, turned on by accident. Hurry, please*! Dragging their hoses, they stormed inside.

Shocked neighbours appeared, strangers too, passersby, and I had to tell the story over and over — *basement, sauna, accident.* More gathered; children excited, *It's her house, wow, through the basement window, see the flames? Awesome!* From inside, smashing, crashing, shouts. Outside, the air reeked of smoke. *Perhaps,* I thought, *this stench on my hair and skin will stick forever.*

Two firefighters appeared, gasping for breath, faces shining with sweat. "It's a hot one all right!" one bellowed to the other, and they stomped back in. Firefighters running up and down stairs, a crowd of spellbound onlookers, and I on the sidewalk, floating above the scene, feeling sick but calm, as if this were happening to someone else. And yet those windows, with their smoky discharge, certainly belonged to my house. Yes, this might be happening to me.

Please let this horrible movie end, I prayed. *Please.* A neighbour told me later that at one point, I swept my arms open high and wide, as if appealing to the gods.

Someone draped a coat across my shoulders, thrust a bottle of water into my hands, brought a chair and urged me to sit. It was comforting to feel my neighbours so kind and close, and yet I'd never felt so alone. Soon this Queen for a Day would be homeless. Homeless.

That summer, my finances were so wretched that I decided to sell my house, a decrepit Victorian semi in a good downtown location. But when my son, who'd lived there nearly all his life and has the house numbers tattooed on his foot, begged me to keep it, I opted instead for a grand money-making scheme: part of the basement would be renovated to rent to a student. I hired a capable young carpenter named Chris, who made some sketches. "No problem," he said, strapping on his toolbelt.

The problem was that the basement resembled an overflowing scrapheap. When Chris saw the mountain of jumble, he laughed. "Who's the pack rat?" he asked. I, said the pack rat. Family and friends kept dying and leaving me stuff, and I saved it all, tons of irreplaceable memorabilia along with my own mementos and regular Goodwill purchases: everyone's yearbooks, bits of furniture, vintage clothing, stacks of records, children's books and baby clothes for my eventual grandchildren, a lifetime's worth of papers. When my brilliant friend Robert died of AIDS, his executors shipped me a box of his writing and photographs; into the basement it went. After the death of my uncle, like my dad a wine connoisseur, a few of his prized bottles ended up with me. Along with everything else, the fine wines were stored in the basement.

In fact, they were stored in the sauna, the perfect place, dark and cool. When my ex-husband and I bought the house, we thought the basement sauna, with its fantasy that Canadian families would get naked and hot and turn into Finns, was an absurd waste of money and space. We rarely used it, and one day I realized that a big box lined with cedar was perfect for storage.

My handyman Len came over to cut the heater wires. He was down there for a long time, muttering "Bastard!" over and over, as he often did. The theatre set designer who'd sold us the house had built and wired the sauna himself, just as he'd installed the dribbling skylights. He was expert at making things look plausible from the front, unused to factoring in rain, or snow, or time.

Len finally stumped up the basement stairs, bushy clouds of hair and beard speckled with plaster dust. "The wiring of a lunatic," he said, "but it's disconnected. You'll never heat your buns in that bastard again." And from then on, the little cedar room was used to put things in.

When Chris the carpenter began work that lovely late summer afternoon, I, cursing my hoarding self, went down into the basement too, my goal to clear out many years' accumulation of mouldering treasure. But I couldn't do it; the towering piles overwhelmed me. Since I wasn't going to get rid of it all like a sensible person, the solution was to push even more into the sauna where I wouldn't have to look at it. Thrusting aside our winter clothing, I piled in boxes and bags until the cedar shelves were stuffed. That collection of mothy quilts — where to put them? Though now the sauna's heating element was just a metal box filled with rocks, I'd never placed anything on top of it before. It still looked dangerous. But it was the only space left.

Back in the main room, I noticed a red light glowing on the wall — the sauna power switch. Had that damn light actually been on, all these years? I switched it off and dove into a box of my great-aunt's piano music, faded sheets of Cole Porter and ragtime. Where to put ... wait, what was that pungent smell? And what ... something strange in the air, little bits ...

"Chris!" I shouted. "Are you soldering something?"

"No!" he called back. "Why?"

My innards froze. A vital shard of remembered information turned my belly to ice. Shoving open the sauna door, I gasped. A four-foot-high blinding tangle of scarlet and heat, snaking up the wall. The quilts were burning.

"Fire!" I screamed. "Fire, Chris! Fire!"

Even as I shouted, I was thinking, *What all living creatures have in common — birth, death, terror before the pitiless might of fire.*

I ran up to the kitchen, grabbed the fire extinguisher — why oh why had I bought the smallest and cheapest? — flew down and thrust it at Chris, who was inside the sauna throwing smoking coats out the door. "I'll get water!" I shouted and charged back up. Seizing our biggest pot, I stood at the sink, frantic, while water sputtered out of the tap.

What I'd remembered a minute before, when still a carefree person, was this: the theatre man who'd built the sauna had accidentally hooked up the power light backwards. When the red light was lit, the sauna was off. When the light was out, the sauna was on. I had just piled quilts on the heating element and turned it on. And it still worked. Len had missed a wire.

Heart hammering, throat dry, I ran down the smoke-filled staircase. Chris's face was white. "Extinguisher's used up. Let's go!" he said, whipping out his phone and vanishing — to dial 911, he later told me. On his heels, I stopped, turned, and choked in disbelief. Already the sauna was engulfed, flames gobbling the walls and ceiling, devouring all those precious boxes and bags and bundles, kindling waiting to burn. The overwhelming heat, the air putrid with smoke, the roar of an inferno gathering strength — how was such instant devastation possible on such a tranquil, such an ordinary afternoon? One moment, I was a humdrum woman cleaning out her basement. The next, I was gaping at disaster.

I ran upstairs and picked up the phone, the air so thick and clogged it was a strain to see those three vital numbers. A woman answered, and I shouted my address. "Fire!" I cried. "Hurry!" As if she might finish painting her toenails before passing on the message. Fleeing outside, I took nothing with me except my own skin.

Nearly an hour later, the firefighters emerged. "It's out, ma'am," said one, lifting his helmet to wipe his blackened brow. I wanted to kiss every one of these heroes, who'd saved my home. The basement of course was destroyed and would need to be rebuilt, but the rest was untouched by fire and would be fine. Life could continue, surely, more or less as before.

"Can I go in?" I asked, and they said, "No, too dangerous," but I told them my purse was in there somewhere. With a fireman behind me, I stepped inside.

And nearly fell to my knees. My cosy living-room — floor covered with muck and mud, rug filthy, sofa and piano askew, coffee table, chairs, and bookshelves upturned, gashes in the walls, pictures and books strewn on the floor. In the kitchen — walls blackened, table smashed, chairs broken, a dark film of ash and water on the ceiling, the floor, on every surface, things thrown down, knocked over, crushed. For a moment I could not breathe.

In our twenty years in this place, though much changed within its walls — a marriage ended, two children and their mother grew up — the innards of the house itself did not change. And then, in an hour, they did.

The fireman said they'd had to chop holes in the walls to be sure sparks weren't still smouldering. I didn't blame him; in fact, I was falling in love with him. The extent of the damage made me want to weep, yet I was focused on my companion, so attractive and big and strong. Such big strong hands, so powerful. I grew aware of my cleaning-out-the-basement clothes, my tank top and grubby shorts.

"I wish I could thank you with a nice cold beer," I said.

"Not while we're working, thanks anyway." He grinned and gave me a mock salute. How could a man look so virile in a pair of giant rubber boots?

I started down the basement stairs.

"I don't know, ma'am," said my champion. "It's pretty bad."

Yes, yes it was. It was rubble and char and foul melted plastic and mounds of black, unrecognizable stuff, brackish, steaming.

Well, I thought, *here's one way to get rid of a lot of junk, fast*. It hurt to recall what those heaps of carbon had been. I couldn't bear to acknowledge that not long ago my daughter, seeking privacy, had slept for months down there, right next to the sauna.

Upstairs, in the remains of my kitchen, I had to lean against the sooty wall, head spinning, to catch my breath. Just that morning, I'd spent hours rearranging furniture. As Chris started his work below, I'd said to myself, "It's never looked better, this house. At last."

Now it could not have looked worse.

But wait, I thought, forcing my trembling legs to move, *look, the floor, the roof, intact*. Here was my purse, undamaged, on the filthy desk. There, the phone book binder with all the important numbers inside. All our photographs, all my work and computer in the home office upstairs, the terrified cat huddled behind a bench outside on the deck, all safe. No one even slightly hurt.

What was gone but stuff? My beloved house was standing as it had stood since 1887. The neighbours were outside, loudly debating whose spare room I should sleep in tonight.

I was alive, with a roof and family and friends. Never more alive than at that moment, standing in my reeking, ruined kitchen, feeling blessed.

Postscript for Crazytime:

Fire: Extraordinarily, the fire was one of the best things that has ever happened to me. The insurance paid for a bright new kitchen with a wall of windows looking out at the garden, and I managed to put in a basement suite that has allowed the house to generate much-needed income.

So here I am, still. Standing aghast in the stinking wreckage, however, I could not have known how well the story would end.

One indelible memory: the following evening, I was in the garden sifting with filthy hands through the charred remains of my possessions when my neighbour Jean-Marc appeared like an angel through the rubble, carrying a tray: a hot dinner and a glass of wine.

The kindness of friends and neighbours was another great gift of the fire.

Among the casualties of the inferno were the vintage bottles inherited from my New York uncle, particularly a Chateau Cheval Blanc, a wine so ridiculously valuable I knew I'd never drink it but instead sell or donate it to charity. It was stored in the sauna, the epicentre of the fire, so was obviously ruined. But I kept the bottle with its burned, blackened label as a souvenir.

Not long after, my dear Lynn was visiting from France. We sat eating her favourite Canadian snack — Cheezies — as we discussed the fire. I got out the bottle of Cheval Blanc to show her and, for the hell of it, opened it. Poured. Tasted.

It was sublime. This wine had gone through the extreme heat of a fire and was still superb, by far the best either of us had ever tasted. We drank the bottle.

With Cheezies.

These essays appeared in:

"Wine Glass, Half Full," *Fresh Air,* CBC, 1998
Stranger on a Train, *Globe and Mail,* 1999
Secret, *Full Grown People,* 2022

COMING THROUGH

It's funny, I always imagined when I was a kid that adults had some kind of inner toolbox full of shiny tools: the saw of discernment, the hammer of wisdom, the sandpaper of patience. But then when I grew up I found that life handed you these rusty bent old tools — friendships, prayer, conscience, honesty — and said 'do the best you can with these, they will have to do.' And mostly, against all odds, they do.

Anne Lamott

WEED

"You want me to smoke grass with you?" I asked, in disbelief.
"Yes, but only if you promise never, ever to call it grass again," replied my daughter, her boyfriend grinning beside her.
"It'll be a bonding experience," said her best friend.
What to say?

The topic of drugs first arose in this very kitchen, when Anna, a curious fourteen, asked if I'd indulged in the sixties. While not actually lying about my own youthful drug use, I'd been as vague as possible in response and hoped she'd "just say no."

She did not. I knew she'd started to smoke weed and tobacco and also sometimes to drink too much. My job was to hover, near yet far, keeping a stern eye on things, letting her know she was under surveillance, but also giving her and her friends a safe place to do what they were going to do anyway.

Maybe that was wrong, too lax. In comparison with some parents, however, I was puritanical. The dad of one of my son's friends used to buy pot for his boy and smoke it with him and his buddies. "He's so cool!" exclaimed my son. His pal did, however, end up dealing in large quantities.

But now these young people are in their early twenties. It's not necessary to maintain an abstinent moral pose; now I do want a bonding experience. Anna is home from university for the summer, but next summer she'll perhaps stay down east and work. Our bonding opportunities are growing fewer. And besides — what can happen?

Of course I used to smoke as a teen. The first time marijuana was presented: It was 1967 and I was sixteen, wearing an orange mini-dress and purple tights, hair cascading down my back, sitting cross-legged on the floor of Tim's parents' house listening to *Sgt. Pepper's* for the very first time. I'd never even smoked a cigarette, let alone an illegal substance, and here it was — grass, weed, pot, Mary Jane — being solemnly passed. How sophisticated, how counterculture. I inhaled and coughed and inhaled again, feeling a bit sick, a bit light-headed. I felt light. I felt. I heard. The music — incredible mind-blowing music!

By the end of the second side, with the orchestra sawing away on that famous ever-swelling crescendo, I was a flower, an eager daffodil straining through the soil and bursting out into the sun.

"So groovy," was all I could say, heart slamming against the orange dress. "Far out!"

One night I rolled a joint and puffed in my bedroom, blowing smoke out the window so my parents wouldn't smell it, before going out to Le Hibou coffee house to hear an unknown young folksinger from Saskatchewan warble for me and twelve other people. Talented, I thought, with a lovely clear voice and long sheets of golden hair. This Joni Mitchell might go far.

My parents, who were cool, finally said they'd like to try this new thing and asked to smoke with me and my brother. We all smoked hash together one night in 1969, while listening to Bob Dylan's newly released *Nashville Skyline*. My mother had a sensational time, chortling and weaving around the room as if drunk. My father sneezed several times. "Well, if nothing else," he said, scowling, "this stuff certainly stimulates my mucous membranes." He didn't like it. "I have my drug," he said, pouring himself a glass of wine.

By the early seventies, I was with him. For some reason, marijuana made me introspective in the most negative way. Instead of a pleasant sensual experience, getting stoned brought up all my failings, losses, stupidity. It felt as if a critical, self-destructive voice emerged from the smoke and attacked.

I quit and had not smoked weed since. My drug of choice was the same as Dad's.

Now, thirty years later, Anna and her team are holding one little joint. I can handle one little joint. I puff, hold it in, pass it on. Puff, hold it in, pass it on. Only three puffs, and it hits. And then I remember, the stuff these kids smoke is not like ours was. In only a few minutes I am very, very stoned. And I am very, very scared. But this time, I can't show anything, must not make a fool of myself in front of my girl and her friends.

Heart racing, I'm hanging onto the chair arms. Someone says, "Yeah, that's great, put that on," and out scrapes the raucous voice of Janis Joplin. Janis Joplin — what decade is this? The room should be filled with incense, and all of us, sitting on a faded Indian print bedspread thrown over an ancient sofa, wearing little round glasses, a curtain of hair, bell bottoms, love beads. Janis Joplin. It hurts to hear her, shredding her vocal cords.

I'm sick with fright. The pit — the pit, the deep dark hole is going to open up and swallow me. It's right there. *You lazy, pathetic specimen of a human being,* the voice begins. My hands clutch the chair as the room spins and my stomach lurches.

But this time, I manage to take a deep breath.

NO, I say to myself. *I am NOT going to fall into that hole again. I'm not twenty-three, I'm fifty-three, I've raised two children, we are sitting in my house. I'm all right. We are all, all right.*

My heart slows. A bit.

Anna and her friends are laughing, chatting, unaware of the battle going on in me. "This stuff is much stronger than I'm used to," I manage to say, trying to laugh with them, forcing myself to drop my shoulders and relax. My daughter says she's proud of me; her brother, away living with his dad, wanted to be the one to smoke with me first. He'll be jealous, she says.

My mind turns to a wondrous moment when I was the age Anna is now and dropped mescaline with my great friend Bob. We stayed up all night. Early in the morning, drifting stoned around the city as the sun rose, I noticed a cobweb studded with dewdrops, a perfect construction drenched with glittering light. It was the loveliest thing I'd ever seen. Kneeling on the ground, I gazed at it for a long time, lost in admiration for the meticulous artisanal handiwork of spiders, for the miracles of nature, for this astounding planet. I have never forgotten that cobweb.

Be here now, we used to say. Peace and love. We were really trying to change the world back then, to make society and people kinder and gentler.

Only we didn't.

Through my haze I hear how hilarious Anna is when she's stoned. The other two are also funny, smart, quick. It strikes me, for the first time, how bright Anna's best friend is; I lean over and tell her so.

Then, "Janis was different from the others," my voice announces. "Jimi, Jim Morrison, they didn't have to die, they were careless. But Janis always seemed to be driving toward death."

"Wow," they say, blinking at me. This relic, this ancient monument, was actually there.

"Do you want to hear about it?" I say.

LETTER TO MUM (NEVER MAILED)

D ear beloved mother of mine:
There was a time, as you know, when that kind of affectionate greeting would not have been possible for me to give and you to receive. A time when my anger at you, and yours at me, was strong. But now my anger is gone, and when mine ebbed away, so did yours.

You're not the mother of my fantasies, a woman wise and supportive who has solved her own problems and so is free to give me my due, to celebrate my strengths even when I'm weak — because I'm her daughter, who will depend on and imitate and need her, always. That is not who we are to each other.

I know, even if you sometimes don't, that you're lucky to have me as a daughter. All my life, I've done my best to support and care for you, and there have been many times when you needed a great deal of support and care. And at last, after a long struggle, I know this: I'm lucky you're my mother. I've learned a great deal from you, and there is much of your legacy I wish to keep.

And there is much I do not. Perhaps this is typical of any daughter. Daughters look at their mothers and think, *That's not how I would live my life. Not how I would treat my partner, my kids, my cleaning lady, my friends. The husbands of my friends. I will be different with my children. I will be different.*

And then that daughter does have children, and suddenly she is her mother. She hears herself speak and thinks, *Where did that voice come from? That's HER voice! That's not the voice I want in my own throat.* But there it is. Because that's the voice we heard for fifteen, twenty years, dealing with husband, household, offspring. When we grow up and start to do the same, that's the voice we hear.

Dear voice in my throat, you've had a lucky life. Yes, there was not much warmth and generosity in the thatched cottage where you were born and grew up, in an English village. You had health problems, a strict schoolmaster father, a very busy mother who was attentive only when her daughters were ill; the family had rigid Victorian principles and no money. Your mother's mother had kept a ruler at the dinner table, to thwack her daughter when her spine was not straight enough as she dined.

But you discovered early how to thrive: you smiled. You were charming, beautiful, and exceptionally tall, with a quick mind and many talents — musical, artistic, athletic, academic. Your stern British parents could never acknowledge your gifts — no praise, no boasting, no self-indulgence allowed. Because your mother's heart had already been claimed by your oldest sister, you went for your dad. He was not a giving man, but he was yours. You weren't the son he'd wanted, but you became his girl. Your poor sister Do, in the middle, was no one's favourite.

You have always known how to attract. It has to do with your eyes — the sweep of the eyelashes, like Princess Diana's, the way you gaze intently and then look away shyly and smile. It's your vocation to make men love you. Now a widow in your eighties, you're still gathering them in.

In 1944, in Oxford, you met a new kind of man: a handsome, dynamic Yankee soldier. To each of you, no one could have been more exotic — for him, a six-foot-tall blue-eyed blonde born in a thatched cottage; for you, the first Jewish person you'd ever met, a New Yorker whose grandfather had been a famous Yiddish playwright. When you followed him to America after the war, his dark-eyed little mother, born in Odessa, hated you on sight. After your marriage and my birth, we moved to Halifax, where I was a happy child until baby brother Mike arrived to displace me.

And then there was the new man, Dad's good friend, the one you left us for, temporarily, after we'd just arrived to spend two years in London.

I don't blame you for leaving. With my own divorce behind me, I know not to judge other marriages. Yours was fractious; you felt unappreciated, embattled, and here was an ardent lover who worshipped everything about you. He left his own wife and children to follow you to England. Mike, who was two, and I, six, stayed in the cold little rented house in Golders Green with my furious father and the housekeeper he hired.

One day when Dad was at work, you rang the doorbell. I ran to you, and you swept me up and carried me away, leaving my brother behind only because he was at nursery school.

So then I was yours, and Mike was Dad's. It was months before we tentatively reunited as a family. When we talked later about this traumatic time, you said airily, "Oh, you were fine. You had me."

What I resented for many years was not that your marriage suffered a crisis, but that you made light of what that crisis meant for me. We'd just moved to a strange, foreign place when one day you vanished, and then, just as suddenly, I was with you, and my father had vanished. After your lover was forced to return to his family, and a few months later you and I moved back in with Dad and Mike, you were still quivery and ambivalent. My life as a marriage counsellor, as a child trying to hold together a disintegrating centre, began then.

The real blow came next: you fixed me to your side and shut Dad out of my life. My brother belonged to both of you, but I was yours, belonging to you alone. That was simply the way it was, always, until Dad died. He and I managed eventually to make a secret connection, but we knew we were forbidden to be openly close. Any closeness, for us both, was reserved for you.

There are other things, many other things in my list of grievances, especially that you continued to pursue or be pursued by a number of other women's husbands, including a second one with whom you had a long affair, devastating his wife, a dear friend of our family. You were heedless in your quest for adulation. But for me for decades, you had no flaws at all. I believed, made myself believe, you were perfect; Dad was the problem. After his death my marriage began to go to pieces, and I floundered as a mother. So I went, finally, to therapy, assuring the therapist my life was wonderful, there were just these few little issues.

"I think you should come back," she said when she'd heard the issues.

"Really?" I replied, surprised. "You think that's necessary?"

We talked for a year before we talked about you. And then the flooding began. She helped me understand how much of my upbringing had been about your needs, not mine; that you'd stepped over vital boundaries again and again. Like the time, on a visit to Vancouver, you insisted that I, just turned seventeen, accompany you in our rental car to locate the mansion where your long-gone first lover lived. We sat outside the gates, you sobbing while I scrunched down, hoping we'd not be seen.

Like the time you wept — you're a major weeper — when discussing the divorce of her parents with Anna, who was ten. "It just devastated me," you cried, and then, seeing her face, you added, "It must have been hard for you too."

Like your critical eye on me as a mother, your disapproval of the way your grandchildren were being raised. You were shocked on one visit to see I'd bought ready-made cookies.

"I'm busy," I said. "Baking cookies is not part of my job."

"Oh but it is," you replied sternly. "It is."

You made delicious oatmeal cookies, no question, my favourites. I'm grateful for them. But perhaps you could have registered that I already had several jobs and was coping alone.

My own fierce daughter would say to me, Suck it up, woman! Move on. You're a grown-up now. Anna says you can blame your parents until you're thirty, and then it's up to you to fix things. I agree.

But still, though well over thirty for the first years of my therapy, I did blame you; not that you had flaws — who doesn't? — but that you hadn't sought help to fix them, to fix yourself. As I grew angrier at you, strangely, I grew less so at my own children. I got better as a mother and worse as a daughter. You were hurt, and I didn't care.

My breakthrough came the day my indignation overflowed. You and my brother had come to see me in Toronto, a disastrous visit. You both accused me of manipulating the writing of my uncle's will, a false, vicious, devastating charge. How could my own family, who should know me better than anyone, think that of me? Weeping, trembling, I wanted to throw both of you out of the house and never talk to you again. Instead, that night, I wrote you a letter incandescent with outrage. Before mailing it I emailed it to an old friend. He called the instant he received it and gave me a lecture about the self-destructiveness of fury. "Your anger hurts only you," he said.

At the same time I read, in a book, "Anger shows you where you're stuck." And understood: I was stuck on the page of your faults, hurting myself with resentment that you were not the mother I wanted you to be.

When my anger receded — not right away, but before long — I stopped condemning you and at the same time stopped needing you.

And now I love you very much. I'm grateful you've passed on to me your skill at making family and guests welcome in a warm, comfortable home. You're an original, vibrant, warm-hearted, with sweetness and a fine sense of humour — like a small girl sometimes, giggling, full of anticipation with the gifts you buy, the treats in store. You've always been generous. As things between us improved, you've become more supportive and appreciative, attempting to understand the problems of my life, that they are different from your problems. Perhaps you've begun to accept, at last, that this mother and daughter are two separate people.

You've always loved me deeply, in your way. That I know, now. There's a reason, despite the pain of aspects of my childhood, that I'm able to love as fully as I do — because for the first years, anyway, you cared for me so well. I thank you for that.

None of this gratitude could have come before I burned through my rage and opened to you. When I did, a new world of friendship was there for us. It's true, we're not living in the same city, and so we mostly talk on the phone.

But I call often, enjoy talking to you, want to hear what you're doing, thinking, experiencing.

Sure, things you say and do still drive me crazy. Your flaws are still evident. Some of the qualities essential in a mother, at least to me, will never be there. Instead of judging, instead of trying to fix you, I imagine myself floating above my frustration and grief, above what makes me cringe, high up there in the pure atmosphere of the love that's been rekindled for you.

Sometimes, to do that, it's necessary to pull my heart way back. Often, as we chat on the phone, I'm doing something else — reading the paper, getting supper ready. What's funny is that I know you are too.

All that matters, Mum, is that I'm doing my best to celebrate who and what you are, rather than resenting what you are not. All you have given me, not what you have withheld.

And my hope for the future is that my daughter, my own stubborn, wise, and loyal daughter, will do the same for me.

SHE LOVES YOU

ate C swung open at 5.30 p.m., and I ran. I sprinted up the hill in a pack of fast movers, all of us shoving past the hapless security guards, who for a few foolish moments thought we'd stand still while they inspected our backpacks. I ran, sides heaving, blood pumping, and did not stop until I crashed into a metal safety barrier and could go no further.

The stage wasn't close, but it wasn't far, either — 120, at most 150 meters straight ahead. The lucky people from Gates A and B, which had opened first, were in front. But then, those lucky people had started waiting at five o'clock this morning. I hadn't arrived at Gate C until just after noon. Thanks to my sprint, I was at least dead centre, in the second row of Section C.

Only fifteen minutes later, the crowd had filled in beside and for countless rows behind me. I'd had a lunatic fantasy we'd all be sitting on a hill; that I'd stretch out the hotel towel I'd brought, and once comfortably settled, would go in search of beer and food and a bathroom. But pushing through the vast crowd to get something to eat or to pee or even to escape briefly from the crush would mean I'd never get back to my precious spot. This was it.

My spirits sank, for the first and last time that long day.

What the hell are you doing here? I shouted silently at myself. *You're a grown-up, for God's sake!* And then, a buzz of joy. Here I was, almost fifty-eight, giving myself license to behave like a teenager, to suffer for love, for art, for music. I'd been waiting outside the gates for more than five hours. It would be another four before the main attraction began.

And then, to celebrate the four hundredth anniversary of the City of Quebec, Paul McCartney — Macca, as we super-fans call him — would sing, for free, on the historic Plains of Abraham.

For me and two hundred thousand other fans packed in on all sides, as far as the eye could see.

I'd never done this kind of thing before, but then, I'd been a single mother with a mighty load of responsibility and little money. It's no coincidence a mad jaunt like this only happened when the kids were launched and their mother was free to leave home herself. Now there was a bit of income and time, not only to travel, but to remember. I liked to remember my time with Paul McCartney. He'd once made me very happy.

In January 1964, listening to my first L.P., *Beatlemania!* with those beautiful faces in half-shadow, I'd adored every song. But the instant a soft, sweet voice began to warble "Till There Was You," my thirteen-year-old self made the most important decision every kid that age had to make — which Beatle?

I was a Paul Girl.

But just as for the first time I was fitting into a gang of kids at my Halifax school — fellow Beatlemaniacs — my father took us away to spend a year in France, where I knew no one. My troubled relationship with Dad was aggravated by our isolation in a foreign country. Many solitary days were spent in my room, scribbling fantasy stories about Paul.

During that challenging, friendless time, my passion for the cute Beatle kept me company. Kept me sane.

The climax of the year came in June 1965, when the Beatles landed in Paris and played a small arena twice in one day. I saw both concerts, barely taking my eyes from Paul and screaming so hard, my throat was raw for days after.

Though records by the Who, the Stones, Simon and Garfunkel, Bob Dylan, and Joan Baez whirled constantly on my record player, the Beatles were by far my favourite until 1970 when the band broke up. In the seventies I was preoccupied with work and almost lost track of them, with their four solo careers. Then came the terrible day John Lennon was murdered, and the dream of a Beatles' reunion died too. But in December 1980 I was pregnant with my first child, devastated, but also sheltered and immune.

My children knew early if they wanted to butter me up, all they had to do was put on *Abbey Road* or *Revolver* or *Sgt. Pepper*; I'd start to dance and sing and say a blissful "yes" to whatever they wanted. Nothing, nothing cheered me up like an old Beatle song — and then a new one too. In the last few years, Paul's stream of fresh CDs featured melody after melody that remained stuck in my brain for weeks. This dazzling musician was once more commandeering my heart. Yes, his second marriage was a foolish mistake, that was clear to the world long before it was clear to him. And perhaps he was occasionally the eager-to-please baby-face he'd always been.

But most importantly, he was a stellar family man and citizen and had never stopped making sublime music. He mattered all over again.

COMING THROUGH

So when I heard about the free concert, I thought, *Why not?* Unlike in Paris, I didn't have to beg my dad to let me go. I could dress for comfort, knowing Paul was not going to see me this time. Unlike at the Palais des Sports in Paris, where he did. I was in the eighth-row centre in my best dress, a baby blue shift, jumping up and down with a big picture of my Beatle. The house lights remained on; no flashbulbs were permitted, so the band wasn't blinded by popping flashes; and strangely, the audience around me consisted almost entirely of older French boys. It's not absurd to believe Paul noticed the girl in the baby blue shift in the eighth-row centre waving a big picture of him, and nodded to her and smiled.

He nodded to me and smiled. I was sure of it. I wrote ecstatically in my diary that if death had snatched me at that moment, I'd have died at the pinnacle of my short life.

Forty-three years later, in order to see him again, I didn't know the wait would be more than nine hours; that I'd have to gallop to get a decent spot; that I couldn't drink anything all day, because it'd be impossible to get to a bathroom. I didn't know hearing Paul's music would rip open my rib cage.

Luckily, I did not know these things and so I went.

The summer of 2008 broke national records for rain, and the city with the most rain in all of Canada was ... Quebec. But for that entire day, the weather could not have been more perfect — warm but cloudy, not too hot with a welcome breeze. The blue-grey sky darkened, turned dark pink, mauve, purple, black. Roadies moved around on stage, provoking roars of excitement. I chatted with my new friends on all sides, especially a young medical student from France.

"Mon favori, c'est 'Yesterday,'" he told me. "Mais 'Back in the USSR' est fantastique aussi."

Next to him, Gina from Lac St. Jean agreed.

"Il est le plus grand star du monde," she said, showing us her T-shirt on which she'd scribbled her phone number, so Paul could get in touch. She smiled warmly at us and then crumpled slowly backwards, still smiling, in a faint. Eventually, she was hauled over the safety barrier in front of us and carted away, her space instantly filled with two others.

At last, at 9:25, there he was, striding onto the stage waving and smiling.

"Bonjour, Quebec!" cried Sir Paul. "Bonjour tout le gang!"

A deafening yell of approval and welcome. He strapped on his guitar and launched into "Jet." And suddenly, two hundred thousand people were singing along with the chorus –"Ooooo." The young Frenchman knew every inflexion, every harmony. "Jet!" the crowd bellowed. But this and the ones Macca sang next were newer Wings songs, not Lennon and McCartney, and I didn't know them well. The Frenchman knew them all.

At last — "All My Loving," the first Beatles classic. Paul sang "All My Loving" in Paris in 1965, and now here we were again, both of us singing, but only one of us overwhelmed and crying. But beaming, mostly. I danced in my squashed spot until a woman grabbed me and told me to stop moving because no one behind could see. From then on, when the need to dance seized me, as it often did, I bent my knees and crouched.

"Blackbird," alone with an acoustic guitar, the vast crowd still, silent. Opening the white album for the first time, pulling out the picture inserts, realizing there were *two* records here — so much Beatle. A lifetime's worth of listening.

He played a game with the audience; he'd sing a series of notes, and the crowd sang them back to him. Like he was in his living room, fooling around with dear friends.

"Eleanor Rigby," "Penny Lane" — the best. Evocative, enchanting songs.

"Something in the Way She Moves," played on George's ukulele and dedicated to George. My year at theatre school in London, 1972, I was in the Down elevator at Harrods when George Harrison got on with a friend or bodyguard. He stood directly in front of me, inches away, with very long hair and moustache, wearing a shaggy black fur coat. Everyone in the elevator, in true British style, paid him no mind; though quivering with excitement, I tried not to either. The doors opened and off he went, my third favourite Beatle.

"When I Saw Her Standing There." I was thirteen the first time I heard it, four years younger than the girl in the song, and Paul was four years older.

He said, "This next song is dedicated to mon ami John." He gestured to the sky, and the entire place erupted into shouts and applause. Tears poured down my cheeks again. He played "A Day in the Life" leading into "Give Peace a Chance."

"Lady Madonna." "Get Back." "Let It Be."

"This is heaven," I thought, no, more to come, one of the loveliest songs ever written: "Hey Jude."

"Sing with me," he said, and two hundred thousand people chorused back "Na na na na," waving their hands in the air. He stopped playing and came to the front of the stage to listen, and we were all singing to him.

I was in a stupor. The band left and came back twice. Paul said affectionately to us, as if speaking to a small child, "You have to go home now. Do you remember home? Where that is?" He sang, of course, "Yesterday," at the piano, and finished hoping we'd enjoyed the show. We're sorry, he sang, but it's time to go.

The love you take, he told us, is equal to the love you make.

It was over, the concert of a lifetime. He'd sung till well after midnight — nearly three hours, thirty-six songs, without leaving the stage. He came on waving a Quebec flag and later in a Quebec sweatshirt, he attempted French with good humour and friendliness, bantering with the audience. At sixty-six, the man was indefatigable, like a gleeful boy, made to perform. His hair was dyed mid-brown, the colour it used to be, and his face was youthful. When he played the piano, though, there was a close-up on the big screens of his hands, and they were sixty-six-year-old hands. In fact, they looked like an old man's hands.

But if he'd been younger, much younger, he could not have given more.

Two hundred thousand people, satiated with song, started to drift home. The rubble of garbage — food wrappers, water bottles — was appalling, but it was a peaceful exodus, people singing, laughing, carrying sleeping children through the elegant old streets of Quebec, past ancient buildings glowing with illumination. I was dazed, hungry, thirsty, incredibly tired. My legs were like wood, my back and bladder ached, I felt I'd been pummeled and was so fraught I kept bursting, still, into tears.

It was hard to comprehend the force of that much emotion in one night.

In bed in the hotel, afloat on a river of music, song after song swirling through my head, I thought about my romantic fantasies in Paris. That long hard year, in the absence of actual love and friendship, I created for myself an ideal mate and companion, tender, devoted, always by my side. Looking back on all my own loving, I realized that, except for the blissful early years with my husband, I'd not ever experienced sustained love for a man equal to the intense bond created with my chosen Beatle.

This was not and is not an imaginary bond. Any relationship between us is of course make-believe, but the power of the admiration, respect, and attachment I feel for Macca and his music is a sustained force and absolutely real.

I'm grateful to have been that young girl whose soul opened to "Till There Was You." To have chosen blindly and yet, somehow, wisely. At thirteen, I embarked on a journey with a big-hearted, brilliant, tireless man who'd accompany me with the gift of music and memory for all the days of my life.

MY FATHER'S FACE: A Visit with Alice Neel

My father was twenty-seven in 1949 when he posed for the artist Alice Neel. A veteran who'd served in a U.S. Army medical unit during the war, he was a handsome *bon vivant* with a salty sense of humour and a voracious love of wine, women, and song. In the portrait, although Neel captured his good looks, his hazel eyes and thick dark hair, she portrayed him as a sombre man in a tie and dark jacket, a pipe clenched in his narrow hand. He paid her $50 for the painting.

Nearly four decades after her death, the Metropolitan Museum in New York produced a huge retrospective of the work of Alice Neel — now considered one of the greatest and most radical American painters of the twentieth century. *New York Times* critic Roberta Smith wrote that the exhibition "confirms Neel as equal if not superior to artists like Lucian Freud and Francis Bacon and destined for icon status on the order of Vincent van Gogh and David Hockney."

Yet for much of her lifetime, this visionary artist struggled to make a living.

In the late 1940s, Alice Neel was one of my father's dearest friends. While Gordin Kaplan was studying for his PhD at Columbia, he, Alice, and her lover Sam Brody were part of a gang of lefty rabble-rousers that included both graduate student scientists like my father and mad bohemian artists like Alice. They were all targeted and relentlessly hounded by Joe McCarthy and J. Edgar Hoover's FBI, to the extent that when Dad received his degree in 1950, he took a job in Canada and never returned to work in the land of his birth.

He carried with him into his new country a treasured souvenir: Alice's painting. She only painted faces she found unusual and interesting, so to have a Neel portrait, even in those days of her obscurity, was an honour.

That portrait hung on the wall of every one of my childhood homes, my father's sober demeanour, pipe in hand, always suspended behind us. He was a man of few possessions. Alice's painting was one of his most cherished.

In December 1980, I flew from Vancouver to Ottawa to visit my parents for Christmas and decided while there to take a quick trip to New York. Thirty years old and five months pregnant, I wanted to do as much as possible before being tied down by parenthood. My life was in a period of unsettling transition; I was in love and leaving the theatre to take a graduate degree in creative writing. Temporarily or perhaps permanently, I was leaving a profession in which I'd achieved success but had long felt was wrong for me, to explore one I was eager to be part of but knew little about. In New York, there were lots of Kaplans to visit, but it also seemed important to meet the artist and family friend who'd laboured in near anonymity for decades before becoming, at eighty, something of a sensation.

Nervously dialling the number Dad had given me, I was relieved to find Alice friendly and welcoming. "I'm Gordin Kaplan's daughter," I told her, "an actress on a brief visit to New York ..."

"Kappy's daughter? An actress?" she boomed. "Come on over — have tea!"

In a squat, shabby building at 107th and Broadway, the door to apartment 3A was opened by a teenaged girl, Alice's granddaughter Olivia. The flat was basic, unfancy, long and narrow with bright windows. The walls, not to my surprise, were covered with art by Alice and others. Lining the halls were rows of unframed canvasses, portraits stacked two or three deep.

Alice was waiting in the living room. She scrutinized me.

"You have Kappy's face," she said, with satisfaction. "It's a wide face; it goes out across here, not down, like your mother's."

What did she mean? Though my eyes are like Dad's, my mother and I share the same long chin. But the portrait painter spoke with authority, so perhaps I'd passed some kind of test. She noted my belly and heard about my pregnancy with no comment.

We sat in the cluttered living room. Alice Neel was not at all what I'd expected. With a generous motherly body and billows of white hair floating about a soft round face, she looked the farthest thing from the activist painter my dad had described — a woman who'd always lived on the margins, who had two sons by different men, neither of whom she'd married. Revolutionary behaviour in the late thirties and early forties.

She asked about Dad, and I told her that though he missed New York a great deal, he was grateful to Canada, which had sheltered him. For decades he'd been a voluble leader of protests against nuclear proliferation and nuclear fallout and then the Vietnam War. She nodded.

"I think I'll see nuclear war in my lifetime, and I'm eighty," she said gloomily. "What a terrible thought. And this new president, I don't think much of him." The month before, to the horror of progressives, Ronald Reagan had won the presidency in a landslide.

"Olivia," Alice said, "dig out that canvas — *The Actor*." She turned back to me. "Aren't you glad to be in the theatre, Beth, not an ordinary mortal? You should be glad, to be so special."

I didn't feel special and certainly didn't feel anything in common with Ronald Reagan; my proudest accomplishment as an actor had been to help form a small communal theatre company that wrote its own topical plays. As I opened my mouth to explain, Olivia brought us a tray with tea and slices of buttered bread and then vanished to another room.

"Kappy was like a bear," Alice said, as she poured tea. "He used to tell stories from the *Iliad* to my son Richard. Richard was only seven, but he remembers to this day. He has a memory like mine."

I wondered aloud if that's why, during my childhood, Dad had chosen as a bedtime story a picture book of the *Iliad*. The stories he read were not only beyond my grasp, they were in French. Recounting this made me chuckle. Not Alice, though. Perhaps that was the Kappy she'd known and painted: a man who'd read the *Iliad*, in French, to a four-year old.

I told her how much the portrait meant to him and congratulated her on her artistic success. "The only secret to success is hard work," she said sternly. "Did you know that? Picasso said, 'I was born with an obsession for hard work.' Very modest of him. Now young painters won't begin until they have a loft in SoHo." Her lip curled in disgust. "A loft in SoHo! In art today, publicity is what's important. I was unknown until my fifty-ninth year, imagine that."

Looking at the canvasses propped against the wall, imagining the decades of hard work that had gone into them, I couldn't fathom the kind of stubborn strength it must have taken, as a woman and a mother, to remain personally and professionally committed to her own unfashionable ethos, not just for a few years but for a lifetime. Recently Alice had been championed by the women's movement for her humanist vision, her realism and craft, and especially for her empathetic depiction of the lives of women and children, but she was still not well off, nor a member of the artistic establishment.

Sipping my tea in the messy room, surrounded on all sides by great art, I was happy to listen as Alice launched into a monologue.

"I was born in a small town. It was so boring I've been making up for it all my life. I've never left New York. Oh the strange people we knew, your parents and I, the artists in The Village. The woman who was deported for having an affair with a dog." She leaned toward me as she exclaimed, "Yes, a dog! She used to smash pill bottles and dance on them."

"I don't know what to make of New York any more," she sighed. "I was held up in this apartment only two years ago. Two young men."

I gasped.

"They ignored all the paintings," gesturing to the work against the wall, "and only took the television!" This time, we both smiled. "I used to be always ignored," she said. "Not like you."

Her glowing impression of my theatrical life made me uncomfortable. My most recent show had been the worst experience yet, a soul-destroying disaster with a venomous director. Alice was peering intently at me again.

"I never liked my face," she announced matter-of-factly. "What a boring face, little round face, a real Anglo-Saxon face. I hated it."

But you have a lovely, expressive face, I thought.

"Now it's more interesting, now that I'm old, and my body is interesting, the flesh falling off my bones. I have deformed feet, you know; they're interesting, my feet. I decided to paint myself in the nude, at eighty. The painting made a big stir. Olivia," she called, "go get the *Newsweek* that has the canvas reprinted."

She swivelled back to me. "I used to sit here naked and paint, and one day I realized a man was standing on the street outside, watching. So I moved. Now I get phone calls. A man just phoned wanting to take a photo of me in the bathtub."

I exclaimed in shock again.

She shrugged. "I said no. Some publicity is good. Some publicity is not good."

Looking at the magazine, the way she'd conveyed the sagging breasts, protruding belly, and strangely twisted feet, I marvelled at the fearlessness it took to paint oneself in the nude at any age, let alone this one.

My hostess said her granddaughter had considered becoming an actress, what did I think of that?

It was finally my turn to rant, to warn this lovely young woman. "It's a grueling way to make a living, Olivia," I said. "I'm trying to get out of the business myself. So much rejection and excess — feast or famine, too much work, then none. Actors are mostly self-centred and deeply insecure, directors can be manipulative and callous, the money's almost non-existent — "

Alice interrupted, her face furious. "What are you saying?" she cried. "Why would you spoil her dream? You're making fun of the theatre. You're making fun of your work! Are you a good actress? You can't be. To me you sound lazy and thoughtless and spoiled. There you sit, complaining. Why aren't you working now?"

She stopped and picked up a slice of bread.

It was as if she'd slapped me hard, taking my breath away. Yes, I wanted to say, I'd been considered a good actress, and now it was my dream to be a good writer. But I couldn't speak. In Alice's tirade I heard my father's voice. During my childhood and adolescence, Dad would often rage at me, accusing me of being spoiled, selfish, and lazy. This woman I'd just met had said the same thing. It hurt beyond measure. What if they were right?

The tea was cold, and Olivia was hovering. But Alice continued as if nothing had happened, serenely offering me a plate.

"Have some bread, Beth. Have some tea. Do you like my new sculpture?" She gestured vaguely. "See that canvas at the end of the hall, there?" I turned to look. "Two homosexuals. One in his underwear, and his lover, not a happy man. I thought it was right to paint him in his underwear. This year he was killed in Puerto Rico, a lover's quarrel. He was in his underwear. Isn't that strange?"

Yes, I agreed, it was very strange.

"You must meet Richard. Olivia, phone Richard."

"Another time, thank you, Alice," I said, exhausted. "I should get going and leave you to your work."

"You must go? We've had such a lovely talk," she said as I rose. "Was I very hard on you about the theatre? I don't like sarcasm. Do not mock your art. Painting keeps me alive. What else is there for us to do?"

What else is there for us to do? I wasn't sure, but I wanted to find out.

"Thank you for making time," I said. "Dad will be very pleased I met you." We did not embrace.

"See that self-portrait by the door on the way out?" she called after me. "It's so ugly. That's how I saw myself once!"

Alice Neel died of cancer almost four years later, on October 13, 1984. I was too preoccupied to register this momentous loss, because that's the day my second child was born.

Since then, year by year, Alice has gone on becoming more famous worldwide. Critics acknowledge that she saw not only faces and bodies but souls and represented them in a way no other artist did, as in her ground-breaking portraits of a scrawny, scarred Andy Warhol or the eccentric writer Joe Gould, whom she painted naked, with three penises. No one saw people like Alice.

Four years after her death, in the summer of 1988, my father too was dying of cancer. Our once fraught relationship had evolved into a bond of great warmth and mutual respect. He'd said how proud he was of me, my family, my writing. I didn't know why he'd made me his scapegoat back then, but the why no longer mattered. Between us now there was, simply, devotion.

A few days before he died, as I sat massaging his feet, Dad spoke about Alice's painting. Because my younger brother had such a rootless, unsettled life, and I did not, after my mother's death, Dad wanted me to inherit the portrait.

Hearing this made my eyes overflow. The painting meant so much to him. In all our years together, this gesture — wanting me to have his portrait — was his most overt expression of love.

But he did not write down that bequest, and so it did not, could not, happen.

When my mother died two decades later, my brother Mike and I were tasked with settling her estate. We didn't get along particularly well, and I dreaded the thought of what we faced, especially dealing with the portrait. I absolutely did not want to sell it — not only a great work of art but my youthful father's soul! But there was no choice; Mike and I owned it jointly and would never agree on what else to do with it. In any case, neither of us had much money. We imagined the Neel would be our fortune, since some of her works had sold for hundreds of thousands of dollars. My fantasy was to use the money to secure my old age and to help my children put down payments on places to live.

I had superb digital copies made and framed, one for me and one for him, and we began the complicated process of selling.

It turned out a small dark portrait of an unknown scientist and social activist, even one painted by Alice Neel, was of no interest to anyone. It went through two modern art auctions at Sotheby's where it was ignored, before, finally, a private buyer appeared. After paying various fees and factoring in our expenses, my brother and I each received $11,000.

The copy, of course, has pride of place on my wall. Dad and his pipe are still there, as they have been throughout my life. But what hangs there is not the real thing, and it makes me sad that his beloved face, as visualized by a brilliant friend, now animates the home of a stranger. My father would be sad, too.

Also left by my mother were stacks of old letters. Going through them, I found one written in 1951 by Sam Brody, father of Alice's younger son Hartley, and was surprised by the effusiveness of his and Alice's affection for my parents. Sam applauds Gordin's "wit, humor, bonhommie," and finishes, "Alice loves you both in a very special way reserved for you alone."

I visualize this young couple — clever, beautiful Sylvia from an English village and Gordin, the vigorous, noisy Yank — breaking bread and drinking wine in Spanish Harlem with the unconventional artist, her Communist partner, and their crazy comrades.

In 1949, the year of the portrait, Sylvia and Gordin would marry. Eleven months later their girl child would be born, a daughter with hazel eyes, thick dark hair, and a forceful chin, who after various turns and twists would grow up to be a writer. A writer who would one day do her best to immortalize them all in words, as the magnificent Alice Neel had done in paint.

What else is there for us to do?

MY BIRDS HAVE FLOWN

My nest isn't empty. It's unusually quiet and neat, the fridge stays full, and the phone hardly ever rings, but it's not empty, because I am in it. My children have left home, for now; the elder is at university down east, and the younger has just gone to live in the States for a few months with his dad. Twenty-two years of parenting, thirteen of those on my own. A long time ago, a friend with two youngsters the age of mine called. "Are you swimming or just keeping your head above water?" she asked wearily. "Or are you drowning?"

I did go under, more often than I care to remember, like the time I ran screaming out the back door into the snow, to avoid throttling my offspring who'd finally, after years of trying, pushed me over the brink of sanity. It's been disheartening to discover how limited, how impatient, spineless, forgetful, fearful, petty, and bad-tempered I really am — uncovering, with pain and embarrassment, the rock bottom of my soul. And uncovering, at the same time, the rock bottom of theirs.

Of course, there have also been countless moments of sweet connection, when love floods my body and I think, *How did I live without this great bond*? Nearly half my life has been spent shadowing these two.

Contemplating those years, I can state honestly that motherhood came hard to me. Raising kids was a job, not a vocation, and I wasn't that good at it. I wanted to sit in silence reading the newspaper in the morning, not make nutritious breakfasts, help with puzzles, squeeze Play-Doh, clamp together Lego blocks. Later, struggle to get two resistant, sleepy young people out the door.

What I really wanted was for my children to sit quietly and read and write, to do their homework and work at healthy time-consuming hobbies, as I recall doing for much of my own childhood. But they had far different ideas, and so we squabbled. I wanted to change them, they had to confront me back, and we all lost. There were times, many times, it wasn't clear we'd come through.

But, so far, we have. This clumsy gardener is watching two scraggly plants strengthen and bloom before her eyes. And the problem is that as these two mature, they're more and more enthralling, not just as my progeny, but as people. They're wonderful company. I want them nearby forever.

But their job is to go away, for good. My job is to prepare them to leave and to make it easy for them to go.

I was able to rehearse for the day my house would be empty of children on the weekends they went to their father. One moment my walls were reverberating with noise and activity — phone ringing, doorbell, neighbourhood kids stomping in, music blasting, the pounding of giant sneakers on the staircase, the shower, shouting.

And then, silence.

I tried to embrace that silence, and part of me actually did. I got a lot of work done. Fat books beckoned me to read. But part of me was in shock or in storage, waiting to emerge again; they would soon be back. Without them, I pursued my adult social life as a single woman, unencumbered. But I was — am — used to being encumbered.

It's hard to imagine the time is near when my much-loved encumbrances will be gone, not just temporarily, but forever.

The plan is to take up all the things I've always wanted to do: learn to speak Russian, travel widely, join a choir. Sink into an armchair and read great fat books for hours at a time, the way I did as a child.

No matter how tranquil and stimulating those days, a piece of me will always be elsewhere, with my children. How is it possible the sound, the smell, the life force of them fills my house and my being, and yet I must shake them free?

Wait a minute. I'm getting carried away here. Rumour has it children don't actually leave home anymore, with tuition and rent so expensive and jobs hard to get. They may simply stay in place for years to come. MY place.

That's another thing entirely. I love my kids, but do I want to go on living with them as adults? Absolutely not. When they're gone, I'll miss them unbearably and insist they keep in regular touch, but I have things to do. And I cannot do those things until there's some time and space around here, thank you very much.

My job for twenty-two years was to be there, a presence in the kitchen, a volunteer in the schools and the community. Rightly or wrongly, the way I thought I could do my best for my two — and their friends, because our home served as a drop-in centre and youth hostel — was by being around, listening, available, there. Despite the difficulties, and God knows there were plenty, my reliable presence in their lives was worth it for us all.

But my career is another matter. What career? I've kept going slowly, very slowly, teaching part-time and writing. Today my offspring, like the manuscript of my book, are out there getting on with the rest of their lives, so it's time for me to get on with the rest of mine. In some kinds of creative work, age doesn't matter, at least, that is my fondest hope. Insight matters, and perspective, and humour, patience, tenacity, courage, drive. These qualities, after raising children for twenty-two years, I hope are mine.

My parent peers and I are the first generation, surely — if we're fortunate enough to enjoy good health — to anticipate another whole lifetime of productivity after our kids have left home.

Whatever a mother chooses to do with her time after having children, I've learned, there are rewards, and there's a cost. Both before and after divorce, I had many lonely, hopeless days, many delightful ones too, and most just treading water. But now my precious offspring have grown up and are moving on. Despite my flaws as a parent, they are — mostly — solid and mature and fine. I'm proud of them, and even better, I like them.

But if these young adults return to live here again, as it's possible they will, things will be different. They'll find their mother attempting to give less and expect more. I've had a taste of life without them, and it suits me.

One of my life's fulltime jobs is winding down. The next has barely begun.

KICKING THE CAR HABIT

D riving my silver hatchback to its new owners, I burst into tears. From now on, my own metal box on wheels would not be there to offer convenience and luxurious privacy. I would not be able to zoom about the city in a bubble of my favourite sounds, in a climate adjusted specifically for me. My frail self would be out in the elements, alone and unprotected.

I almost changed my mind and turned back.

The grateful new owners drove me home. A young couple originally from Bosnia with a small child and complicated work schedules, they needed a car far more than I did. In anticipation of their gain and my loss, I'd motored around the last few days, getting in heavy things — bags of birdseed and potatoes, a futon I'd managed to cram into the back. Because from then on, buying birdseed and futons would be considerably more complicated.

I'd like to say my decision to get rid of my car was simply to help save the planet, but it's not true. First, I was no longer needed as shuttle bus driver for my kids and their friends. Since my days as a chauffeur were over, the expense of maintaining this vehicle was increasingly hard to justify. The cost for me alone was way too high.

In any case, my house and job are downtown. Although the hatchback was parked on the street outside, I often left it there and walked half a block to the streetcar. Yes, partly to save the planet, but mostly because parking was so difficult and costly and driving so bloody infuriating. I was enraged all the time at aggressive, thoughtless smartphone-jabbering drivers, giant show-off SUVs, stupid, thoughtless parkers taking up more space than they needed. City driving was bad for my peace of mind. And to visit elsewhere in Ontario, it was easier to get the bus or train, to put up my feet and arrive rested.

The last straw came the second time someone smashed a side window in the middle of the night. Enough, I decided. Time to try living carless. But for a while after the sale, I felt vulnerable and hard done by, convinced getting rid of my vehicle had been a big mistake.

Luckily, I'm a huge fan of bicycles, one of humankind's greatest inventions. Despite the constant danger — I was hit once by a car — zooming about the city on my powder blue bike fills me with enormous pleasure. How gratifying it is to pedal past a line of steaming automobiles caught in a jam. If it's a bad day for biking, I take the streetcar or subway and use the wait time to read and people-watch. And after calculating the thousands saved each year by not owning a car, there's no guilt in treating myself regularly to cabs, often, in the bargain, plunging into conversation with new immigrants to this country.

When a car is essential, it's easy to get one, thanks to AutoShare. Like its rival Zipcar, this nifty organization has cars parked all over the city, allowing its members to slide behind the wheel of a vehicle not long after deciding to rent one. Yes, it's not my very own silver steed waiting at the front door. There are days — snowy or rainy days, plain weary days, any day in February — when I long to just slam a car door and turn a key, safe and warm. My shoulders ache sometimes from the tension of biking, avoiding lethal car doors, streetcar tracks, and careless, aggressive speeders. There are friends in the far reaches of Toronto I rarely see now, because it's just too hard to get there. To visit a place like the McMichael Gallery north of the city feels like an adventurous trek to the Arctic.

The good news is that I've discovered an effective new diet: the Carless Weight Loss Plan, which involves getting trim and fit by biking, walking, and carrying potatoes and birdseed home in a backpack. It's a boon to shop almost exclusively in my own neighbourhood, and a relief not having to maintain an incomprehensibly complex machine.

Life, for this downtown resident, is blessedly simpler without a car. I have not only saved money, I've saved energy, tranquility, and time.

And also, in a very small way, this beautiful, generous, patient, depleted planet.

LAVALIFE

S ome time ago, I decided to try to meet men virtually. Internet dating was just starting to open up, and single women were flocking to give it a try. With a great deal of difficulty and care, I wrote a humble-brag advertisement for myself:

"I'm fit mentally and physically, active of body and brain, a writer who teaches writing and has been working for many years, on and off, on a book. That's why I haven't dated much since my divorce — I've been home with the kids and the book. But now kids and book will soon be gone, and I'd like companionship and more.

I'm tall, a left-wing optimist and good listener, a former actress who was voted "Best Legs" in high school. I'm addicted to red wine and dark chocolate, books, most magazines and newspapers especially the New Yorker, junk stores, my regular fitness class at the Y, and old episodes of Seinfeld and The Simpsons. My favourite men currently, besides friends and family, are Johnny Depp and Nelson Mandela. I love Vermeer, Kandinsky, Matisse, and David Milne, Bach, Beethoven, Prokofiev, Blue Rodeo, and of course the Beatles. I like walking, dancing, biking, sightseeing, travelling. My massage therapist says I have the body of a twenty-five-year-old. My heart is also twenty-five. My face is considerably older.

My dreams, besides continued health, world peace, and the defeat of George W. Bush: to have written a good book, to learn to speak Russian and go there and to many other places (Newfoundland, the Queen Charlottes, the Grand Canyon, Japan), to make more time for music, to see all the good films I somehow missed, and to spend part of the year by the sea, whether the Atlantic or the Aegean. I dream of a vibrant lover, friend, and partner with some hair on his head and some intellect inside it, interested in joining me on some of those ventures; a tall, open-hearted, connected man who knows how to laugh, think, and talk, and who makes the effort to understand himself and this difficult and glorious world."

Before submitting this masterpiece, I responded to a Personal ad in the newspaper and met up with a man who in no way — mentally, emotionally, and especially physically — resembled how he'd described himself. Though he was eager to pursue a relationship, I decided the need for a partner wasn't that pressing; I had things to do, places to go, books to write. The Lavalife ad was put away forever, along with the desire to seek out strangers to date.

Several friends have met life partners on dating sites; I'm happy for them. Others have wasted many hours in hopeless encounters.

I have not.

As for what I wrote then, Johnny Depp was a favourite because the amusing *Pirates of the Caribbean* had just come out, but he'd not be on my list now. The Queen Charlottes have become Haida Gwaii and I still want to go there, and to spend more time by the sea. I did take a few Russian lessons in anticipation of a trip there to explore my Jewish roots, but in the world as it is these days, Russia is not a place anyone wants to visit.

My ad now would be very different. But I'm not going to write it.

Postscripts for Coming Through:

Letter to Mum: *The last two years of my mother's life were difficult. Leaving her apartment as it was in case she changed her mind, we finally moved her to a pretty, if small, one-bedroom suite in assisted living. But she kept falling, going to hospital, coming out, going into hospital again. She was losing memory, often weak and vague; I kept flying to Ottawa to tend to her. Once I had to make a choice between Anna in hospital with her newborn, who had croup, and Mum again in hospital. My brother had phoned to say, "This is it, get here quickly!" Abandoning my daughter, I chose my dying mother, flew, rented a car, drove like crazy.*

When I walked into her hospital room, she was sitting up in bed, beaming, drinking a cup of tea. I almost killed her myself.

That summer, Anna and I twice brought her new baby to Ottawa so Mum could meet her great-grandson, but she wasn't much interested. "Babies are so boring, aren't they?" she whispered to me. In the last good photograph of her, on Thanksgiving in October, she's wearing blue, as she always did, and doing a crossword puzzle. As she always did.

My mother died in hospital two months later, at 3 a.m. on Christmas morning. She was eighty-nine. I will always be sorry no one was there with her. But during our talk on the phone two days before, she'd made clear she was very tired and wanted to go home.

I asked Anna not long ago if she'd come over to help me sort out my office, overflowing with paper. She took one look at the piles and stacks and stuffed file drawers and sighed. "Mum," she said, "if you don't deal with all this, SOMEONE ELSE will have to."

We both knew to whom she was referring. I spent days and days in my mother's apartment after her death, dealing with her massive quantities of stuff. I may do Anna a favour and deal with all this, yes. Or perhaps not. I have a lot to do and not much time, now, for sorting. When I die, the plan is that she'll inherit enough money to hire someone to help with the tedious work.

For now, I sit surrounded by comforting nests of paper and memories, as my mother did.

Miss you, Mum.

She loves you: *Now in his eighties, Macca is still making new music and doing three-hour concerts. During the pandemic lockdown, he recorded an album of his own songs, playing all the instruments himself. Recently he's been writing children's books and publishing his photographs of the sixties. He's a creative phenomenon.*

I cannot imagine the world without him.

COMING THROUGH

Kicking the car habit: *Shortly after this piece appeared as an op-ed in the* Toronto Star, *a flurry of emails expressing great interest landed in my in-box. It turned out readers thought the Carless Weight Loss Plan was an actual method I'd invented for losing weight and were anxious to know more about it.*

They were disappointed to learn what the plan entailed: they just had to sell their car.

These essays appeared in:

Weed, *Globe and Mail*, 2004
My Father's Face, *The New Quarterly*, 2021
My Birds have Flown, *Globe and Mail*, 2004
Kicking the Car Habit, *Toronto Star*, 2008

ARE WE THERE YET?

To grow up costs the earth, the earth. It means you take responsibility for the time you take up, for the space you occupy. It's serious business. And you find out what it costs us to love and to lose, to dare and to fail. And maybe even more, to succeed.

Maya Angelou

If you have a garden and a library, you have everything you need.

Cicero

READING HARRY POTTER

Now that last week's hype about the release of the new and last Harry Potter novel, *Harry Potter and the Deathly Harrows*, has died down, I've enjoyed the welcome sound of millions of minds reading. There hasn't been that intense a silence since the last time a Potter book came out.

Two years ago, puffing around the running track at the Y, I was joined by a friend, a dignified Porsche-driving advertising executive with grey hair and beard. He was anxious to talk.

"So who do you think the half-blood prince is?" he asked, and gave me a list of his theories. I didn't agree with any of them.

As we jogged around, we did not pass the time complaining, as usual, about our almost-grown-up children constantly in need of money. We weren't moaning about the demands of work, our aging bodies, the unpredictable weather. No, we were debating whom Hermione will end up with.

"I rather thought that she and Harry would ... you know ..." he said.

"God no, absolutely not," I protested. "The chemistry is completely wrong! It's got to be Ron."

When *Harry Potter and the Half-Blood Prince* came out, life slowed down for a while.

My son Sam was nearly twenty-one back then. He'd spent many of his teenage years lying on the sofa clutching a computer game control, using his thumbs to play violent contact sports or steal cars in Las Vegas. Or he was watching fifty channels simultaneously, or chatting in cyberspace and checking out God knows what websites. Then suddenly he was six foot eight, a skilful waiter in a trendy restaurant.

And this sophisticated youth with tattoos and a seven-second attention span was thrilled that on the Saturday the new *Harry Potter* was released, he had an early shift. After work, he galloped home from the bookstore where he'd preordered his copy, made a nest for himself on the deck with comfortable chair and vat of fruit punch, and plunged into the book. He didn't stop reading even for supper, this young man who's always hungry. Only when his phone rang to summon him to a party did he stop, and even then, he wanted to take the book along to read on the subway. "Not a good idea," I said. "You might lose it."

As soon as he left, I grabbed it and began to read. Twenty-four-year-old Anna, meanwhile, in her apartment across town, was reading her roommate's copy. When she came over to eat and do laundry and borrow money, she gave me some advice. "Mum," she said, "when you get to the part in the book where Dumbledore and Harry go on a trip together, make sure you clear yourself some time and just read through, okay? You won't want to stop." She was right, I didn't, and managed to fly through that bit before Sam reclaimed his book.

The next night, my street was blacked out by a fallen hydro pole. A neighbour couple sitting on their porch in the dark invited me to join them. I told them I was hurrying home to read *Harry Potter* by candlelight. They were incredulous. "You're wasting time on popular children's junk?" the husband cried.

"Actually, J.K. Rowling is a superb writer," I said. "It's not her fault she's a blonde kajillionaire."

"I saw one of the movies," said the wife. "It was silly."

I left them there and went home to find a flashlight so I could read in bed. Sometimes things are really good even if they're popular. The movies might be disappointing, but only because the books are so much richer. Rowling has reminded us that the imagination behind our own eyeballs paints much more vivid pictures than film's most expensive special effects. She has rekindled the simple magic of sitting alone with a book in your hands. I adore her for that.

And for the fact that as a single mother, sitting with pen and notebook in a café, she invented a world of such depth and complexity that my adult mind has to strain to catch the details. And that she has given me, a fellow single mother, an experience and a world to share with my almost adult children.

Sam finally relinquished the volume to me, and I cleared my agenda for the rest of the day. Picking up the book and sighing with contentment, I was a child again, poring over *Little Women*, weeping as gentle Beth died. I was holding *A Little Princess*, Nancy Drew, the mesmerizing Narnia books, *Alice in Wonderland*, *Charlotte's Web*, *The Borrowers*, the Hardy Boys, *The Secret Garden*.

I was ten years old, curled up in the big armchair in the living room, so immersed in imagination that when my mother called me to set the table for supper, I looked up in bewilderment, unsure of where I was. Just as my son did that first Saturday with *The Half-Blood Prince*, as he unfolded his very long frame and, blinking, looked around.

I sat on the deck and read till the end. The kids had warned, "There will be tears," and sure enough, there were. When Sam came home that night, we had a long talk about what might happen next. We ran our thoughts by Anna, who'd been impatiently waiting for us to finish. The three of us, independently, had come to the same conclusion about Snape.

There were tears this week, too, about the end of series: after *Harry Potter and the Deathly Hallows*, there will be no more. When we've finished this one, we'll be ten years old one last time, surfacing from an enchanted world, looking up and wondering where we are.

TURNING SIXTY

My father was only sixty-five when he died. He was a francophile who, as an American soldier housed in a Parisian convent toward the end of World War Two, had fallen in love with everything French. He especially adored French wine, great Burgundies that until the last years of his life he could not afford to buy. He would croon the velvety names like incantations — Chambolle Musigny, Nuits-St.-Georges, Gevrey Chambertin. Afflicted with stomach cancer, he mourned the cellar stash of wine he could not drink.

During our last Christmas dinner together, the rest of us sampled vintages from his *cave*. My father struggled to sip a glass of water.

Next year, decades after that mournful Christmas, I face the big six-oh. Thinking of my dad's too-early death, I wonder how many years are left to me. Perhaps it's my luck to inherit my mother's longevity genes, but perhaps not; sixty-five is looming, an iceberg on the horizon, an ominous marker. Most of my big life changes, tidily for someone born in 1950, began at the end of each decade: in 1969, becoming a professional actress; 1979, leaving the stage, marriage, motherhood; 1989, divorce, intense therapy, becoming a writer. In keeping with tradition, 2009 is the year to celebrate a life change, a year to take stock.

Once the grand adventure was figured out — five months in Europe, to include the wedding of my goddaughter, Lynn's Jessica in Provence — arrangements fell into place. I was able to negotiate a five-month sabbatical from teaching, and the mother of a friend rented me her small *pied à terre*.

Later this spring, I will hand the keys of my house to the Dutch family who rented it over the Internet and fly, on travel points, to Paris. As I wander around the City of Light, retracing the paths I walked so long ago, the ghosts of my father and of my own young self will be walking there too.

Over four decades ago, during the year we lived in France, Dad wanted to share with his family the riches of his beloved city. But he couldn't appease me, his surly daughter, furious at being uprooted and determined to hate everything.

Sure enough, our first months there gave me plenty of reasons to be miserable. Unable to speak a word of French except merci and s'il vous plait, I stumbled through my first weeks at a forbidding Parisian high school, indignant, lonely, and scared.

Before long, however, the countless pleasures of the City of Light opened to me. I began to spend blissful Saturday afternoons wandering along the Boulevard Saint-Michel in the Latin Quarter, admiring the suave garçons on their Mobylettes, the sleek-haired girls whose knee socks matched their poor boy sweaters. Only a few months into my school term, I was fluently bilingual. This apprehensive small-town Canadian was soon at ease on the Boulevard Saint-Michel, wearing her own striped poor boy sweater and devouring a *pain au chocolat*.

When I step off the plane, the words of that once-incomprehensible language will flow from my mouth, thanks to Dad.

But although some reminiscing is inevitable, this journey is not about nostalgia. It's designed to help make a dramatic delineation between my first five decades — my old life — and the one beginning now. I want to prepare myself for the years ahead. My life in Toronto is crowded with the busyness of work and home, friends and neighbours, my mother's needs and my kids'. In Paris, I know four people, none of them well. This is my chance to shut up and shut down. Like so many others, I've chosen that glorious city to escape the familiar, figure out who I am now, and write.

Like Joni Mitchell, I will be a "free man in Paris;" like her, I hope, "unfettered and alive."

For sure, I'll be as lonely and frightened sometimes at nearly sixty as at fourteen. I'll wonder what the hell I'm doing. What the hell *will* I be doing? Traipsing through countless museums and browsing in the bookstalls along the Seine, as my dad did with me. Sitting with Waterman pen and Clairefontaine notebook in Aux Deux Magots, pretending to be Simone de Beauvoir. Receiving helpings of inspiration and enlightenment along with my *steak frites*? I hope so. Who knows?

This April I'll arrive as a woman who's spent decades raising children, researching a book, and teaching. Now, at last, the children are adults, and the book is published — wait, let me say that again, the book is published! And my other responsibilities will have to get on without me for a few months.

Soon after arriving, I'll go to a bistro and order a glass of good wine, in honour of Dad. There is no better place to drink a toast than Paris. *L'chaim*, as the Jews say. To life. To love. To health.

My own health is fine at the moment, touch wood. I can see and hear pretty well, my teeth are still there, and so, perhaps, is much of my brain. It's time to find a new purpose, launch a new stage of life. Now.

My father's glass of water haunts me.

HANDBAG ON THE TRAIN

There are moments when time stands still, and the heart stops. Today, it was my heart that stopped. But as you see, I'm alive to tell the tale.

Almost at the end of a marvellous, once-in-a-lifetime, five-month-long stay in France, I got on a train. An acquaintance leaving on vacation had sent me the key to her empty apartment in Montpellier and invited me to move in for a week. At 7:15 p.m., after a long journey, I got off the train and walked out of the Montpellier station heading for the apartment, towing my wheeled suitcase, backpack on my back, planning what to buy for dinner.

And then, in a blinding moment of nausea and panic, I realized I did not have my handbag. I did not have my handbag. It was still on the train.

How much can flash into the brain in an instant. In the handbag: my wallet with all my money and credit cards. My passport. The keys to the flat in Montpellier. My camera, address book, and phone.

Screaming "No!" aloud, I ran, flying back into the station to find the train, which was going on to Marseilles. Maybe it'd still be there. I couldn't run fast enough with my suitcase, so charged into the magazine store, dumped the case by the counter shouting, "*Je retourne!*" and ran out again, with the woman crying after me that it was forbidden to leave bags anywhere. I tore down the stairs and up to the platform. The track was empty.

No train. No train. No handbag. My mouth was so dry, I couldn't swallow and wanted to be sick. I walked back, retrieved my suitcase with the woman still shrieking about terrorism, and found the Acceuil, the office that handles traveller's problems. Luckily two officials were still at work. I blurted out my problem: no money, no cards, no key, no phone, no nothing. Night coming on. No one to call.

"The train is non-stop to Marseilles," the man shrugged. "Nothing we can do, madame." He scrawled some big numbers on a piece of paper, as if for a child. "This is the Lost and Found in Marseilles," he said. "Call when the train gets in and hope someone has turned it in."

And he went back to reading. His solution for me: to somehow call Marseilles, to somehow get there if my bag had been found. No help at all. *Thank God*, I thought, *I speak French. What if I couldn't?*

I refused to go away, as he so clearly wanted, and continued to stand there. "I have no phone and no money, how can I call? What should I do, monsieur?" I repeated, nicely but firmly. "What should I do, I'm alone and penniless." The men in the office said they'd contact the controller on the train, but fifteen minutes later, as I sat in desperation and it got darker outside, nothing had happened. Where could I go for help? I knew no one here. Was there a Canadian consulate in Montpellier?

Then by chance a uniformed man who was obviously a big honcho arrived. I cornered him and poured out my story, and he put things into motion. They called the train. Luckily I could remember: car 15, seat 54. I could remember the clothes the woman opposite me was wearing and the little girl on her lap; we'd smiled at each other several times. Would she have noticed the bag? Would she steal the bag? Would someone else steal the bag?

Or maybe I didn't do this stupid thing, I thought suddenly, *maybe I'd dropped it coming out of the station* ... No, I remembered putting my handbag down on the seat behind me while I shrugged on the backpack and pulled down my suitcase. I was thinking about the woman with the restless child, how sorry I was for her they had another two hours of travel. And I'd turned and walked away.

The news came, at last: the controller had found the bag! Incredible relief. I didn't know if my wallet and other valuables were still in it, but he'd found the bag.

They told me the last train of the day was leaving in an hour for Marseilles, I should get that train. "I have no money," I said. They printed me a ticket. I asked them to please fill my empty water bottle, and they gave me a bottle of cold water and lent me a pen, as I had no pen. I understood from them the train got into Marseilles at quarter to midnight, and the Lost and Found closed at midnight.

"What if the train is late and the office closes?" I asked. "I'll be in Marseilles at midnight with nothing."

"N'inquietez pas, madame," said the man. Don't worry, lady. Easy for him to say.

With an hour to wait and no money for food, I wanted to go to the bathroom yet couldn't use the one in the station because it cost fifty cents. But the McDonald's across the street had free wifi — the first and I hope only time my heart has burst with joy to walk into a McDonald's. I used the bathroom, got my computer out of my backpack — thank God that was with me — and emailed my children in Toronto and my best friend Chris far away in Vancouver. If this Canadian was found homeless and babbling, wandering the streets of Marseilles, they'd know how it happened.

The train pulled in, and I got on. They'd given me a first-class ticket. Such kindness — I could not have appreciated more the quiet luxury of first class, the nice big seats. And looking more closely at the ticket, I realized the train got in at 10:45, not 11:45. Lots of time to get to the Lost and Found. My only concern was whether my valuables would still be in place.

As we pulled out of Montpellier, there was the most glorious sunset, a wash of streaky pinks and blues, mesmerizing. And I remembered the other times when my heart stopped. The worst was when my dad called to say, "They've found something, and it's not good." When I was delivering Anna and the doctor suddenly could hear no heartbeat. "Let's get this baby born, now!" she cried, and I pushed with all the strength on the planet. When bad things happened to my kids; events around my divorce. Those were the times that mattered. This was only stuff. This was not health, not love, not life and death, only carelessness and stuff.

Still, my friends, I was one happy woman when the man at the Lost and Found office in the Marseilles train station brought me my handbag, and everything was inside — passport, wallet, cards, phone. "Vous avez de la chance," he said. Yes, I am very very lucky. Thank you. Merci beaucoup!

Now, get this: I went straight to the Acceuil in the station to enquire about trains back to Montpellier the next day, and then left to find a hotel, clutching my handbag tight, tight to my body. Outside the station, I realized I'd left my suitcase in the Acceuil. I was concentrating so hard on my handbag, I'd forgotten the suitcase.

It's definitely time to go home.

It was 1 a.m. before I collapsed in a shabby but clean Marseilles hotel room. The first thing I did, after devouring the almonds always in my purse, was to get out my computer, write this story, and post it on my blog.

Because that's my job.

OPENING MY HANDS

Sitting on the bed in the hotel room, staring out the window at the rusty fire escape, I sip water to wet my dry throat and try to calm my thudding heart. Notes beside me, I whisper my talk to myself for the hundredth time, taking peeks at the paper to be sure nothing has been left out.

I'm about to deliver the Wexler Lecture in Jewish History at the Jewish Community Centre in Washington, D.C., and I am terrified.

What awaits me tonight is the nightmare audience I envisaged all the years of work on my book: a roomful of scholarly Jewish intellectuals. Surely there's no group in the world more critical, with analytical techniques perfected over centuries of Talmudic study. This august group, attending the eleventh year of the annual event, will be expecting the usual prominent scholar, delivering a lecture weighty with research and theory.

And instead — me. An imposter disguised as an academic, because although I teach at two Toronto universities, I'm not a tenured professor but on contract to their departments of continuing education in the flaky world of creative writing. Disguised as Jewish, because, although my father was Jewish, he wanted nothing to do with any religion, and my mother was Anglican. So I'm not officially Jewish.

Yes, I'm the author of the book I've been invited to speak about, *Finding the Jewish Shakespeare: The Life and Legacy of Jacob Gordin*. It's the biography of my father's grandfather, a playwright with a titanic personality who wrote scores of plays produced in New York and then all over the Yiddish-speaking world, including one called *The Jewish King Lear*. I began research over twenty-five years ago and am proud of the book that resulted. But still, I was floored when the producer of these annual talks invited me to Washington, sent a plane ticket, and paid for a hotel.

Surely she'd made a mistake. Surely a chatty, personal talk about my great-grandfather and his life is not the kind of thing her audience will expect or appreciate. I've been struggling to gain acceptance for the book from academics; now here's a unique opportunity to convince them of its worth. If my talk fails, perhaps the book will continue to sink. Have I devoted over two decades to a losing proposition, a 250-page biography no one wants to read?

So I am pacing about the room in my one respectable suit — from Goodwill — incredibly nervous, thinking, *Who do you think you are? You're a fake. This will be a disaster. They'll hate* —

And then I stop. Just stop.

Wait a minute, I think. *I worked hard on the book, and I've worked extremely hard on this lecture. I've done my best. All I can do is hope they like it. And if they don't — it's a shame. But I can do no more.*

Why have I set up an enemy, a wall of critical faces? The audience wants to hear a good story, wants me to succeed. Why invent criticism and shut myself down? How is the world a better place if I am silent? Silenced?

I'm offering them something of value, the gift of my thoughts and words and work.

And standing in the hotel room, I open my arms, palms up. Here it is, my gift to you.

A moment from the past comes back. At a party, with the help of a glass or two of wine, I felt for the first time how painfully tight and restricted my shoulders were. Lowering them, I made myself relax. How much easier it was to breathe without tension. Remembering that feeling, I realize, *When you're relaxed and open, you're not just giving, but receiving.*

That evening, walking out on the stage, I'm still nervous, heart pounding, mouth dry. But I'm also eager and energized, not condemning myself to failure. I take in the audience, rows of intimidating-looking men, yes, but friendly faces, some women and young people too. Briefly, so only I know, I take a deep breath and open my hands toward them. Imagine, all these people have come to hear me. What an honour.

And then, with a good story to tell, I start talking and continue for more than an hour.

They line up afterwards to buy the book — we sell every copy on hand — and the producer tells me it's one of the best lectures they've ever had.

Now when I'm nervous about public speaking, I take a moment in front of the audience. *It's not about you,* I tell myself. *You have a job to do. You have something to give, so make sure they receive it. They're waiting. Give them your gift.*

And I open my hands.

MANIFESTO TO MY FACE

The other day, my friend Kay and I were discussing facelifts. I told her how disappointing it was that a movie star who'd always seemed intelligent and independent has had a facelift or four, and now, like all the others, resembles a blank, serene Martian.

"Women who've had lots of work done don't look good, they just look bizarre and expensive," I said. "You'd think she, of all people, would have refused."

"Ah, but she was a beauty first and an actress second," said my friend. "Aging is much harder on those who were beauties."

Fantastic, I thought. *One aspect of aging I don't have to worry about.*

Though Kay, still a beauty at sixty, is an actress who makes a living with her face, she told me she'd never have it lifted. One day, she said, when directors want to cast a woman with authentic looks, she'll be the only one her age, at least on this side of the Atlantic, who has not been carved into an expressionless moon.

I told her I too will never have a facelift, because of seeing Arthur Miller's play *The Crucible* at the age of twelve and hearing the hero, John Proctor, refuse to sign a false document, even to save his own life. "Why will you not sign?" his family pleads.

"BECAUSE IT IS MY NAME!" he roars.

His words burned into me then and surprised me by returning now. I won't be smoothed and improved, I told Kay, because it is my face. But as the words left my mouth, I wasn't sure what they meant.

After Kay's departure, I went to the bathroom to frown at myself in the magnifying mirror, as it's my habit to do daily. All very well to refuse beneficial surgery, when all I could see, illuminated for my viewing pleasure, were the crevices and splotches of age — the drooping pouchy cheeks and neck, the age spots and moles, deep carved lines and jowls, sprouting chin and upper lip hairs, and bizarrely, considering that I'm in my sixties, the blemishes. Pimples and wrinkles, fighting for space on my face.

Gazing in despair, pulling my cheeks and hairline back and up with both hands to imagine what it'd look like tight again — impassive, flat, younger — at that moment, for the first time, I paused. *When, ever, have you looked in the mirror and liked what you saw?* I asked myself.

Let me think.

There were times, yes, like the day of my eighteenth birthday, when for some reason I glowed with particular force all day long. The early days of my marriage and after the births of my children, when what was reflected in the mirror was a contented woman, brimming with love.

But after pulling out those memories, I couldn't go much further. Except for some special occasions here and there, that's about it. I've spent most of my lifetime looking into the mirror in dismay.

I am not and have never been what you'd call a beautiful woman. I'm not ugly, and my eyes are nice, but the proportions are a bit off — chin too long, cheekbones too well hidden, lips thin, and my nose — well, my first boyfriend called it a lump of melted Plasticine, perhaps with affection. Another boyfriend told me I had a Communist face, and I knew exactly what he meant. And a third said he found me irresistible because I didn't let being plain stop me from living an interesting life. Yes, there's a serious issue with my early choice of men, no question.

What would it be like to walk into a room, just stand there, and be admired? Instead of having to be amusing and smart and *au courant*, to sparkle for your bit of attention. Sure, my beautiful friends don't have easy lives; there's a price to pay for beauty. Just once, I would have liked to pay it. Instead, all my life, I've looked in the mirror and wished to see someone else.

But the other day, with "Because it is my face" ringing in my ears, I contemplated that familiar reflection in the bathroom mirror and thought, *You're getting old, honey, and what you see will not get prettier. Are you going to go on fretting about what is?*

Imagine, looking at myself with scorn during my teens because I was a 32A when the desirable female body was a 38DD. Once breasts appeared, small but at least visible, then for years I despised my body because of its baggage, expanding and shrinking up and down ten to thirty pounds, not acceptably skeletal, like Twiggy's. I didn't see the strength and grace, the creative power of my woman's body, or the glossy auburn hair and smooth skin, the eyes full of humour and curiosity. All I noticed was what the magazines didn't approve of.

And when life stabilized and included healthy food and exercise, so weight was no longer that much of an issue, then age became the issue. Except during my two pregnancies, when it didn't matter how I looked as long as I was healthy, what drew my disapproving attention was the bulge over the waistband and then the increasingly crinkly skin.

What a waste, I thought, standing in front of my magnifying mirror. All those years disliking what I saw; what I am. Wishing to see, to be someone else. Let's start now, I said to myself, accepting, no, cherishing it all.

I cherish you, Face, I said. There's loveliness in your openness and empathy and warmth. You have carried me through all the days and nights, as have you, Body, phenomenal machine beneath my head, still blessedly healthy and resilient, whom I cherish too. The miracle of all those infinitely complex moving parts, still functioning after so many years. Despite the decades of conditioning forced on every first world woman born in the twentieth century, I will try very hard never to say or think anything negative about you again.

For how much longer do we have on our voyage together, this face and this body and I?

COFFEE SHOP AGREEMENT

A summons arrived in the mail, requiring me to go to my children's school for a meeting. My ex-husband, Eric, received one too. I didn't even want to be in the same room with him. Our divorce two years before had started fairly amicably but had descended into warfare.

At the school, we arrived separately and sat on opposite sides of the office. The principal swivelled his head from him to me. "I'm sorry to tell you," he said, "that both your children are in trouble. They're disorganized, angry, and miserable, and they're failing."

My ex's face grew pale and pinched. I was trying not to weep.

I remembered a cautionary tale my cousin, a lawyer, had told me. When friends of his embarked on a vicious protracted divorce that was terrorizing their children, he'd pulled the couple into his office. "Sit down," he snarled at the startled pair, "work something out, and do not get up until you have. Grow up and face your responsibility to your kids. Fix it now!"

Hearing that story, I'd felt disdain. How could a couple willingly damage their children? That would never happen to us. And yet it had.

After six years with this man, I remember clearly the instant, one cold New Year's Day, when I snapped awake. What he and I were living wasn't a fairy-tale romance between two kindred souls, a myth I'd desperately hung onto. It was an ordinary marriage with big problems that needed to be resolved: childcare and chores, time and money. He and I, from very different backgrounds, did not speak the same language about many things; vital words like "budget," "weekend," and "family time" had very different meanings for him and for me. But we never tackled the job of clearing up our disparities. I hoped our problems would just go away, and he perhaps was too busy to notice there were any.

He'd come home late, drained, wanting rest and tranquility, a retreat to give him strength to return to his professional battles. Instead, he walked into

BETH KAPLAN

an old house filled with two normal, noisy, messy children and a frazzled wife. Because I understood so well the demands of running a theatre, I never insisted he make time for us. Later, I realized that if I'd asked him to slow down, to come home, I'm sure he'd have done his best to comply; he loved us and wanted to be there for us, but he was programmed to put work first. And I did not ask, did not know how to ask.

Somewhere, it was my belief this was what marriage should be, he the provider and she the caregiver. After all, that's what played out in my own home, all the years of my growing up. After marrying my father in 1949, my clever British mother, who during the war had helped crack German submarine codes at Bletchley Park, never again worked for money. I'd always sworn to be the opposite of my mother, and yet, in many ways, I turned into her.

A few crises finished us off, including a crush I could not keep secret. After the painful end of his first marriage, Eric had no patience with my infatuation. We argued often. My crush did not abate. Already exhausted, he couldn't resist taking a second huge job.

He gave his soul to the office, and I gave my heart to someone else. The night we finally said, "Enough," such relief flooded my body, I thought I would float away.

Relief, followed by panic. After Eric moved out, I was left grappling with turmoil and fear. Cordial enough at first, he and I fought through our lawyers, not about child support, which he paid reliably and without hesitation, but about spousal support — money to keep a single mother afloat while she figured out her place in the world. Two formerly reasonable people wound up in court, he convinced I was self-indulgent, shiftless, and greedy, and I, that he was bitter, punitive, and blind.

And then came our meeting in the principal's office.

As Eric and I left the school, before we could get into our separate cars, I thought of my cousin's words and said, "Let's go for coffee." He immediately agreed. As we sat down in a nearby coffee shop, I wondered how to begin. It was hard to look across the table at a man who'd once been the centre of my world and was now cool and distant. But underneath, surely, he was still more or less the person I'd fallen deeply in love with. And because we knew each other so well, I was pretty sure he must feel the same about me.

We'd profoundly hurt each other, both of us at fault. But all the trust and compassion we'd once shared couldn't simply have vanished. *Somewhere beneath the wounds*, I thought, *we both still care*. Most importantly, beyond all else, we wanted the best for our children.

"Like it or not, Eric," I said, "we're bound to each other for life. Let's fix it now."

So began the challenge of setting aside years of resentment, anger, and pain to negotiate. Talking and listening for the first time in many months, we arrived surprisingly fast at a compromise about custodial arrangements.

Another coffee, this time with doughnuts, and we tackled the tougher issue of spousal support. For the first time, I who hate thinking about money was straightforward about the minimum I needed, he about the maximum he could afford, and we settled on a number both could live with.

When we shook hands and smiled, I began to breathe again as a whole human being.

After all the thousands spent on lawyers, the solution we'd arrived at in an hour at a coffee shop proved durable. Our frustrations did not vanish — we'd divorced for a reason or two, after all — but we were able to remain tolerant and receptive. Eric found a way for us to hang onto our house, the kids' primary residence, so they kept their home, their school, and neighbourhood. Before long, he and I were able to call and email regularly about our daughter and son, an open line of communication that was a lifesaver when we had another kind of nightmare on our hands — teenagers.

Our divorce was a wound that bled in me for years. The two of us lost each other, and then we lost so much more. But when we made the leap from war to peace, when we transformed from adversaries to child-rearing partners, we earned a great deal back.

Twenty years after that vital day in the coffee shop, our daughter Anna gave birth to a son, our first grandchild. As soon as he could get away from his demanding job in the U.S., her dad flew in to visit. It was thrilling to give him a tour of the garden, which has bloomed into beauty in the decades since we bought the house.

That evening, our son came over after work, followed by his sister with her hungry newborn. Six-foot-four-inch father and six-foot-eight-inch son hovered over the barbecue, and as we ate rare steak and grilled vegetables, we toasted the newest member of our family. A neighbour took a photograph of us, four grown-ups, our arms around each other, with the sleeping baby in the middle. Then the three young ones went back to their own homes across town, and the tired new grandfather climbed the stairs to the guest room, to sleep.

That weekend, my ex and I spent three companionable days under the roof of our former marital home, welcoming the firstborn of our firstborn.

Our daughter began the job of raising the next generation with both her parents by her side.

Before he left on Sunday evening to fly back to his other family, Eric spent twenty minutes straightening my tangled watering hose, the sort of task that used to drive him mad. I showed him a once spindly plant, a William Morris heritage rose, now bursting into astonishing peachy blooms. Saying goodbye in the garden that has taken so long to grow, my ex-husband and I held each other tight for a long moment.

"Much love," I said, as he walked out the door.

And there is.

A LIFE OF WORDS

I t's 3:30, and I'm sitting in my office, where the afternoon sun comes in. There's sun on my face right now. The room is warm, though outside, everything is coated in a foot of fresh snow.

I'm not used to working here, in this very long, very narrow, south-facing room tacked on to the back of the house. But recently, my second-hand store was selling a very long, very narrow desk. Now there's a workspace that fits.

Just now I wasn't writing but reading and compiling. A stack of previous drafts of my current project, a book of essays, is scattered on the desk, but I wanted more raw material so opened a wooden box where some of my diaries from adolescence are stashed.

Pulling out a yellow Hilroy scribbler, I read a bit from 1967. Oh God, that poor girl, so intense, so articulate and insecure. She wrote everything down, every feeling, confusion, crush, a million moments of anxiety or sadness. There she is on page after page, my crazy self at sixteen. Unbearable to read.

The scribbler goes back in the box, lid shut tight. Here I am in the sun. How did I get from there, that imaginative, tormented girl, to here? This relatively tranquil woman. This grown-up writer.

I've always been a writer. Since learning, at the age of six, how to join letters together to make words, it's been automatic for me to put my thoughts on paper. I love paper, love the motion this pen is making right now: the swirls and stems, the black script where before there was nothing, the meatiness of text. The power and mystery of this process: thoughts, ideas, feelings, pouring through my nervous system, through the narrow tube of plastic and ink, scribbled along a blue line on a compressed substance made of wood and rags.

People have been doing this for thousands of years. Now they do it with a tap tap instead of a scritch on papyrus or paper, but the result is the same: thoughts on the page, whether to share with others or not. That is what writers do.

Writer Colm Tóibín once said he had an urge "to communicate levels of feeling — things from the nervous system, and from memory, to other people ... In the same way as when people went hunting many thousands of years ago, someone stayed behind to paint the hunters on the walls of the cave. It's a mysterious thing because it really has no material value."

Understood, Colm. We're painting the hunters and the animals on the cave walls, leaving a trail of red handprints. We were here. This is what we saw, what we knew. Don't forget us.

But it has taken this writer a long time, a lifetime, to get to here, to this place of focus and momentum and even, yes, confidence.

I'm in my house, this much-loved shelter co-owned by the bank and me. Anna and her delectable little boy have just been to visit, to eat and play and pick up a backpack of presents. We had lunch and then they left to go back to their place across town, only a block from where her brother lives. Sam called today too, to share his struggles and triumphs; we made a date for him to come and cook me a gourmet dinner, which he enjoys doing, and his mother enjoys too. I don't think I nagged either of them too much this time or was too intrusive. I'm still struggling to be there but not too there.

Now alone again, as needs be. The office looks out over the garden, where the birds fly to the feeder and back to their nests in the ivy, the birds that are another of my responsibilities. Dorothy would approve. If only she were here to see.

My job, back to work, reading pages of the manuscript, then bits from previous drafts to slot in. For once, the cat is fed, the fridge is full, the plants are watered, the snow is shovelled, the laundry is done. The bills are under control, more or less. Teaching and editing work is up to date. The bed is made.

My heart is at home.

But wait. A long list of boring but urgent errands is hounding me. As always, incessant worries — money, time, health, work, family — roil underneath. I'm officially a senior. Sometimes getting out of a chair, or looking at myself in the mirror, hurts.

But my face is in the sun, writing spread out in front of me. May the pleasure of this work never end, until I do.

Postscript for Are We There Yet?

Handbag on the train: *Travellers' tip #4652: Always travel with a cross-body handbag.*

DO NOT TAKE IT OFF.

These essays appeared in:

Reading Harry Potter, *Globe and Mail*, 2007
Opening my Hands, *Brevity Nonfiction Blog*, 2022

HOW DID IT ALL TURN OUT?

My marriage [is] the ghost that will always haunt my life. I will never stop grieving for my long-held wish for enduring love that does not reduce its major players to something less than they are.

Deborah Levy

As a writer, you are free. You are about the freest person that ever was. Your freedom is what you have bought with your solitude.

Ursula K. Le Guin

STATUS UPDATE

'm now seventy-two. Even putting that number down on paper is hard, because it sounds so impossibly ancient. And yet, like so many other elders, I feel the same inside as I ever did. Leonard Cohen once said, "I'm seventy, not old but in the foothills of old age." He said he hadn't much time to get his songs down and kept going, putting out his last album a month before he died, at eighty-two. Inspiring.

Leonard was good-looking until the very end, as some fortunate men are. In my own foothills, I may feel younger than seventy-two, but I do not look younger, and my body does not function as it used to. It's all very well to write, as I did here, that I'll no longer critique my face, but it's also true looking in the mirror can make me wince. Some women my age appear younger than they are, even without surgery. Your faithful correspondent is not one of them. There are crevices in my cheeks and forehead, new moles, skin tags, and age spots every day. When rising from a chair, I try not to make what a friend calls "old people noises," but it happens — the grunt that escapes as the joints creak and resist. Much time is spent before the magnifying mirror with tweezers, plucking, plucking. How cruel that as we women age, we grow hair in unpleasantly visible places, such as my upper lip.

I recently recoiled, looking at myself in the harsh light of a Zoom call; afterwards, I found the magic thingie that softens your image on camera and turned it up as far as it would go. I look better on Zoom now. Too bad we don't have one of those for real life.

All this moaning about age aside, I have been and continue to be exceptionally lucky in health, and do not for one second take that luck for granted. Like my mother, I have osteoporosis, but although it will never improve, the crumbling of my bones, thanks partly to the Y, seems at least to have stabilized. After my appendix disintegrated a few years ago, I didn't even require an operation to remove it; they healed me quickly with antibiotics. Teeth are all there, reading glasses come from the dollar store, vitamins D and C and fish oil are my only medication, I'm more or less the right weight. Mostly more.

For now.

It's asking for trouble to sound smug. Mum had breast cancer, my father died of stomach cancer, various relatives of other cancers. Most frightening of all, Dad's mother had dementia and chatted daily with her buddy Lawrence Welk on the television screen. When I teased Dad that he might follow her, he replied, "I've got news for you, my dear. Alzheimer's skips a generation." Maybe he wasn't joking.

The Flying Fickle Finger of Fate is hovering over my head. How long before it points at me?

But so far, so good.

How else am I lucky? Doing part-time work I still love after nearly three decades, teaching people how to tell their stories. And of course, I continue to write, although my writing has made little money. Much of my income comes not from my four previous books or from a small teaching salary, but from being a landlady, renting out part of the house. More luck, to have hung onto this house and made it pay.

My kids live so near and yet so far, on the other side of town. A Canadian friend's grandchildren live in Sweden; I remind myself of that when taking the long streetcar ride over for a visit. Sam and Anna, in their late thirties and early forties, both live contentedly on the edge of poverty, in small apartments near each other.

When Anna was eighteen, we took a trip to London to stay with a friend of mine. Our very first night, she disappeared for a walk and came back two hours later; she'd gone to a pub, met some kids and been invited back. In the country less than twenty-four hours, she'd made friends.

Right then, I knew it was time to stop fretting about her. We cared about different things and behaved in different ways; that I knew. What I realized in London is that she's thoughtful and adventurous, resilient and kind, and that wherever she goes, she'll find company.

Later, in her mid-twenties, Anna apologized to me, admitting how vile she'd been as a teen. I guess with her dad not much around, she had only me to battle to become herself, and battle she did. I was no match for her; this mother was a spineless pile of mush. But at the same time, everyone who knows her understands that my daughter is an exceptionally powerful force of nature. Sam said once, "If you'd been stronger, Mum, you and Anna would have murdered each other." And that might be true.

Anna also told me how I could have controlled her teenaged self, and I pass along this vital bit of information for parents of teenagers. She said that if I'd threatened to dance in front of her friends, she would have done anything I wanted.

So simple. Who knew?

She grew up to be a dedicated social justice warrior passionately involved in many good causes. A single mother herself, she's attentive, loving, yet strict with her two sons, generous and open with neighbours and friends. When we argue about certain issues, she is so far to the fiery left that I, in the centre-left making the case for tolerance and perspective, feel like a staid matron — Barbara Bush in pearls.

Despite some differences in our politics, she's one of my dearest friends, a wise old soul I turn to for advice, someone to whom I'd entrust my life.

As one day, we both know, I may have to.

Sam was a bartender for fifteen years, once voted the "Second Best Bartender in Toronto," skilled at the exhausting work of animating a room and making everyone feel welcome. But he has had some nasty blows, a few truly traumatic life experiences foisted on a sensitive man. In his early twenties, he was asleep one night when his best friend overdosed accidentally nearby; Sam woke to the horror of his friend's death and has blamed himself ever since. A tragic number of his colleagues in the restaurant business have committed suicide. At work one day, he heard shots and ran out to find the owner of the bar next door slumped on the steps, victim of a Mafia hit. The bloodied man died in Sam's arms.

Recently, my son faced his alcoholism and began a new life of sobriety. His courage, famous sense of humour, and long list of loyal friends have helped him prevail and triumph. He knows everyone; it's impossible to walk a block with him in his neighbourhood without stopping six times to chat. He too is an aficionado of second-hand, like his mum. Also tattoos, horror movies, video games, and animal skulls, unlike his mum. He daily sends funny texts and links and is still more pensive and vulnerable than many of the women I know.

Bandit, his part-Husky rescue, is the handsomest good boy ever.

Objective observers, people not related to me, have said these two are fine, solid, kind human beings. We speak all the time of our love for each other. Although they are absurdly different in many ways, including physically — he six foot eight, angular, and fair, she five foot five, *zaftig*, and dark — and drive each other crazy sometimes, they have always, without hesitation, been there for one another.

There are lots of worries, as Sam grapples with a complete change in his lifestyle, Anna's energetic boys barrel into their teenaged years, and the planet erupts and floods and burns. These are not easy times.

The kids' dad lives with his wife and young daughter in the States and has a top-level, time-consuming job in a big theatre. They don't see him often but speak regularly on the phone. His Canadian children know he's busy, he will always be busy, but he cares. He loves them.

So, these are, I think, some successes. Looking at the span of mid-life, what are my failures?

Well, I'd like to be more involved in social issues, as Anna is, doing something hands-on and practical to make the world, or just my community, a better place. Even at this age, however, I can barely keep up with my day-to-day responsibilities, so there's little time, now, to volunteer. But many students have told me their work in my courses has helped them deal with their lives, so that's something.

My greatest regret is not having built a life with a partner. Not with my ex — despite our affection for each other, that was never going to work — but someone else. Since my last short-term boyfriend returned to his homeland, there have been a few men, and women too, who've signalled interest, with no reciprocal heat on my part. I've not attempted a relationship, haven't even been on a date, for almost twenty years.

Is something wrong with me?

My dearest friends are divided into two camps: the Terminally Marrieds, and the Terminally Singles. The couples who've been together for many decades, like Lynn and Denis, I find incomprehensible, cannot fathom a lifetime with the same person always there. Of course, it must be reassuring, enriching, to have a constant companion who knows you so well. Matches like the Obama's or Jimmy and Rosalynn Carter's look like stellar partnerships of great mutual benefit. A writer friend told me that after many years, her husband is still someone she loves to talk to. Partners in a good marriage, she said, help each other become better people.

Hearing this made me want to cry, because the absence of that bond is an eternal ache. The early years of my marriage were so fulfilling and joyful. Scanning the obituaries in the newspaper, I read, over and over, "Loving wife for four wonderful decades..." "Dearly missed by her husband of fifty-eight years ..."

The word "we," used so casually by those in a pair-bond — sometimes it lands on me like a blow.

But before I get too sentimental about couples, let me ask, is it not extremely limiting to be in a tight circle of two, chained together as "we," forever gazing inward at each other?

I will never know. I'll never be a widow or leave behind a widower. Someone was quoted in the paper as saying, "The foundation of a successful marriage is a love so deep, it hurts." Hooray — one pain I won't have to feel.

The Terminally Singles, like me and my gay best friends Chris and Bruce, have usually been in one long-term relationship, but after its demise and a few short flings have been single ever since. What is it about those in couples that's different from us? Partially luck, meeting the right person at the right time. Having the confidence and courage to seize an opportunity for love when it presents itself, instead of running in the opposite direction.

More, perhaps it's their ability to accommodate, to be flexible and compromise. Compromise surely is essential in coupledom. A writer once brought up "the personality tithe of marriage." That is, what percentage of your personality are you willing or required to give up — to tithe — to remain coupled? A great deal, for some. Not much, for others. None at all for those of us outside the relationship circle. There's a reason the number of unmarried people in our society continues to rise.

The terminally single women I know are self-reliant, unwilling to bend or admit vulnerability. "Happiness belongs to the self-sufficient," said Aristotle. And who are we to argue with Aristotle?

"I can love me better than you can," sings young Miley Cyrus. Not the best mating call.

Instead of one partner, I have many friends. Through the years, people have told me, "You have a gift for friendship," and I guess it's true. Where did that gift come from? My mother had very few close friends because she considered almost all women to be rivals for my father, including, unfortunately, her daughter. Dad had three or four special buddies, mostly from his youth and in other countries, but was so busy he rarely saw them.

I have good friends near and far whom I care for and keep in touch with assiduously. This is partly out of necessity, for survival; without friends, I'd be lost. They're needed for many things, including, very often, practical advice; for help, comfort, laughter, for a kind word when down. Survival.

There's another once-important facet of my former life that has vanished: sex. I dislike the word "celibate," which reminds me of Catholic priests; we know how that story often ends. But yes, for years I've been intimate only with a nice person who can love me better than you can: *moi*. My libido, blessedly, has shrunk. I laugh to remember once, Chris and I talking about both of us being celibate. But then he began to tell me about his sex life.

"Wait," I said. "What sex life? You said you're celibate."

"Beth, I'm a gay man!" he protested. "Of course I have sex. I'm celibate because I only have sex with strangers, not with a partner."

Ah. Got it. We define our terms differently, my friend.

An added benefit of not struggling any more to emit the pheromones of sexual attractiveness is not giving a damn about the anxieties that plagued my younger years: weight, clothes, hair, how do I look, do they like me? Who cares? I call my closet The Museum of My Clothes, because much of the time, especially since Covid, I'm at home, braless, in comfortable sweats. I can clean up nicely if required, but always with the understanding that no one is looking at me, and I'm looking for no one.

What I miss much more than sex is having someone to share in the endless chores of this house, to help shovel the snow or drag home the heavy bags of birdseed or remember to change the furnace filter. Someone besides my children, cat, and tenants to express concern when, for example, I stagger to Emerg with a ruptured appendix.

But what I miss most without a significant other is ease of travel and exploration, which, ironically, I didn't find even in marriage. My neighbours Jean-Marc and Richard cycle constantly around the city to explore different corners, go hiking or to street festivals or to new museums or parks. They take long trips to distant countries — not long ago a breathtaking voyage through Asia, and then through the length of California. I do not do those kinds of things alone.

After my long stay in France in 2009, I did travel for some years when the winter teaching term ended in March, going to stay with Lynn in Provence, with other friends in France, England, and British Columbia, or touring Spain and Italy with knowledgeable Bruce as my expert guide. One year, however, an exciting new destination: a friend gave me the key to her little apartment in Prague. When I arrived by train from Berlin, it was raining, and I could not remember how to use the key fob to get in. Panicked, I stood outside in the rain for some time before a tenant arrived and showed me how to tap the fob on a nearly invisible side panel to open the door. My friend had given me a list of the best beerhalls, and a more adventurous, less cowardly woman would have been happy to go. But I just did not want to venture out alone, at night, to a Czech beerhall.

Prague showed me the limits to solitary travel in my sixties and beyond.

HOW DID IT ALL TURN OUT?

Despite these grumbles about my life's constraints and the weight of lone obligations and decision-making, I celebrate the fact that as a singleton, I'm free every day to do whatever I want whenever I want, without negotiation or judgment. I set the agenda and am the president, vice-president, and secretary of Beth Kaplan's Life of Surface Brilliance Inc. No arguing or concessions or checking in. There are no consulting partners.

Raymond Carver's beautiful short poem, A Late Fragment, asks if you, the reader, got "what you wanted from life, even so." The answer:
I did.
And what did you want?
To call myself beloved, to feel myself
beloved on the earth.

Yes.

Perhaps my obituary will say, *"She was loved and will be missed by her children, grandchildren, friends, students, and cat. Readers liked her books. Her garden was a haven."*

And that's enough. More than enough.

Right now, it's a good life, hard-earned. For better or worse, I live it solo.

ACKNOWLEDGEMENTS

thought a compilation of mostly previously published essays would come together in a flash. Instead, it took years of wrestling with selection, structure, and order. I am profoundly grateful to all the patient readers who listened to me gripe and helped me cope. My love and thanks:

To my home class students and friends Brad, Curtis, Diana, Jennifer, Kathy, Mary, Peg, Ruth, and Sam, and to all my writing students who inspire me with their courage and commitment

To dear friend and writing colleague Judy and to all my fellow writers in the Creative Nonfiction Collective

To the editors, publishers, and radio hosts from long ago and recently, like Tom Allen, Katherine Ashenburg, James Carson, Susan Scott, Karen Levine, Moira Dann, and others.

To Ellie Barton, the superb editor whose sharp eye jabbed in just the right places, and to Patrick Pearson, tech wizard, who keeps me afloat

To John Sinclair, financial wizard, who keeps me sane, and to the Y that's vital to us both

To Mosaic Press's Howard Aster, who said yes

To Macca, who has kept me singing for nearly sixty years

To my dear friends Lynn and Denis, Ken, Toronto Lynn, Eleanor, Chris, Bruce, Monique, Anne-Marie, Jean-Marc, Ted, Margaret, Penny R., Harriet,

Lani, Suzette, Jessica, Nick, Ed, Tara, Carole, Ron and Babs, and my daughter-by-another-mother Holly

To Mary, a friend in need, a friend indeed.

To friends who are no longer here: Dorothy, Len, Bob, Barbara, Penny H.

To family who are no longer here: my mother Sylvia, father Gordin, Uncle Edgar, Aunt Do, and Pop.

And most of all, always, to my Toronto family — Anna, Sam, Eli, and Ben. I'm proud that you, and these words, are the legacy I leave behind — my red handprints on the wall of the cave.

Onward.